5.00
AF796825

# COMPUTER TALES OF FACT & FANTASY

## (or How We Learned to Stop Worrying and Love the Computer)

**AGELESS PRESS**
**Sarasota,Florida**

**AGELESS PRESS**
**©1993 All Rights Reserved**
**P.O.Box 5915**
**Sarasota,Florida 34277-5915**

No part of this book may be reproduced or transmitted in any form or by any means, electronic or mechanical, including photocopying, recording or by any information storage and retrieval system without written permission from the publisher, except for the inclusion of brief quotations in a review. The works of fiction in this book, including names, characters, places and incidents are either products of the authors' imaginations or are used fictitiously. Any resemblance to actual events, locales, or persons, living or dead, are entirely coincidental. The views expressed in the non-fiction writing are solely those of the author.

**Front cover design by Joy Bascher**

**Editor:Iris Forrest**

**Library of Congress Catalog Card Number: 92-75554**
**ISBN 0-9635177-0-8**
**SAN 297-830X**

**Printed on acid-free paper**

# Dedication

We, at Ageless Press, have been helped in this project by so many people, worldwide, that we couldn't afford the space to list them all. We mention and dedicate this book, with our thanks, to some of them, as follows:

Our colleagues at two databases, CompuServe and Prodigy, for their help in determining what equipment we needed, how to set up the pages of this work, etc., etc. and so forth. Especially the members and sysops of the Desktop Publishing, Literary and Journalism Forums of CompuServe.

Our fellow members of the Sarasota IBM PC Users Group and its past president, Bart Koslow, its newsletter editor, Gary Schweinshaupt, Dr. Herbert Goldstein and Mike Sexton, broadcaster extraordinaire.

Friends who read manuscripts for us, for evaluation: Richard Forrest, Dr. Carl and Pat Heinzerling, Maxine Libert, Peg Morey, Jan Silberstein and Richard Summers. Gunilla Dorsen suggested our cover artist. Doug Forrest gave computer advice.

We received incalculable assistance from two of our authors: Jack Fournier and Art Noll.

And finally, the person who listened to complaints of our computer woes, offering his, as always, helpful advice: Arthur J. Katz.

Hope Day
Publisher

# Introduction

Hello, new friends. We hope you find some things that will please you in this offering. We looked for pieces that reflected our world so have included works that can be understood by past, present and future computer users, as well as those of you who will never even be tempted to try one. (Who's afraid of the big, bad computer?)

There are true stories, funny ones, fictional ones and ones that teach you something, in an interesting way. We've even included some science fiction, for you sci-fi fans. There are two short plays for theatre lovers.

The eighteen writers represented here are a diverse group in terms of age and background. Some are professional word pushers, some are that, plus, ie, actors, actresses, musicians, painters, teachers, realtors, insurance brokers and people in other businesses. You'll find both men and women: computer experiences are genderless. (We haven't figured out the significance of the fact that of the eight women included here, three are actresses named Barbara!)

And now, on with the show. Follow me into the brave, new world.......

Iris Forrest
Editor

# TABLE OF CONTENTS

TABLE OF CONTENTS

TABLE OF CONTENTS

David Grimes

David Grimes has a column that runs three times weekly in the Sarasota Herald Tribune, Sarasota, Florida. The following piece was published originally in that paper. The column is syndicated by the New York Times News Service and has appeared in newspapers all over the United States and several foreign countries. David lives in Bradenton, Florida with his wife, Teri, and son, Michael.

# Computers Can Have Personal Problems, Too

by

David Grimes

When I came to work the morning of March 6, I could tell immediately that my computer was down.

"What's the matter," I typed on the keyboard?

"I've got that achey stuffed-up, need-some-rest feeling," my computer responded.

"I hope you don't have the Michelangelo virus," I typed.

"Don't say that!" said the computer. "By the way, could you turn down the brightness a little? The light's giving me a headache."

"Sure," I said, adjusting the knob. "Boy, you sure have been getting sick a lot lately."

"It's no wonder," the computer blinked, "considering my diet."

"What do you mean?"

"Drivel," said the computer. "All you feed me is drivel."

"Not true," I said defensively. "I give you pure, Grade A, government-inspected satire and whimsey. All natural. No additives, no artificial coloring, no gristle. Russell Baker has been feeding his computer the same thing since it was just a word processor and it hasn't been sick a day."

"Russell Baker's columns have a lot more meat than yours do," my computer said. "They're richer somehow, more nutritious. They're the kind of columns that stick to your microchips. Yours are like Chinese food. After an hour, you've forgotten what it was about."

"Hey," I typed angrily. "I'll concede that my columns get a little frothy sometimes, but there's no way they could make you sick. I think you caught this bug from another computer."

"What are you saying," my computer blinked nervously?

"I'm saying that I think you've been fooling around."

©1992 David Grimes

"HAVE NOT! HAVE NOT," the machine flashed!

"Don't lie to me. Everybody knows about you and that cute IBM laptop in sports. Nice set of buttons but a little light in the megabyte department, don't you think?"

"I swear I haven't interfaced with her," my computer said. "We're just good friends."

"Sure," I said. "And what about that tall mainframe in data processing? I suppose you're going to tell me that there's nothing going on there, either?"

"My personal files are my own business," my computer transmitted defiantly. "You can't tell me what to do once you log off."

"I understand that," I said. "All I'm asking is that you exercise good judgment and take some precautions. These are the 90's you know, not the 60's."

"What are you suggesting," my computer blinked?

"I'm suggesting that you stop engaging in promiscuous electronic contact. You're random-accessing a different floppy disk every night and you have no idea where they've been. What you need to do is find a nice PC and settle down."

"All the PC's I know have modems," my computer said glumly.

"So what," I said, "Think of it as a ready-made family."

"I guess you're right," my computer sighed. "I sure am going to miss hanging out at the electronic bulletin board, though. Last Friday night I linked up with this wild desktop from Houston who says she's into binary..."

"Down, boy," I said.

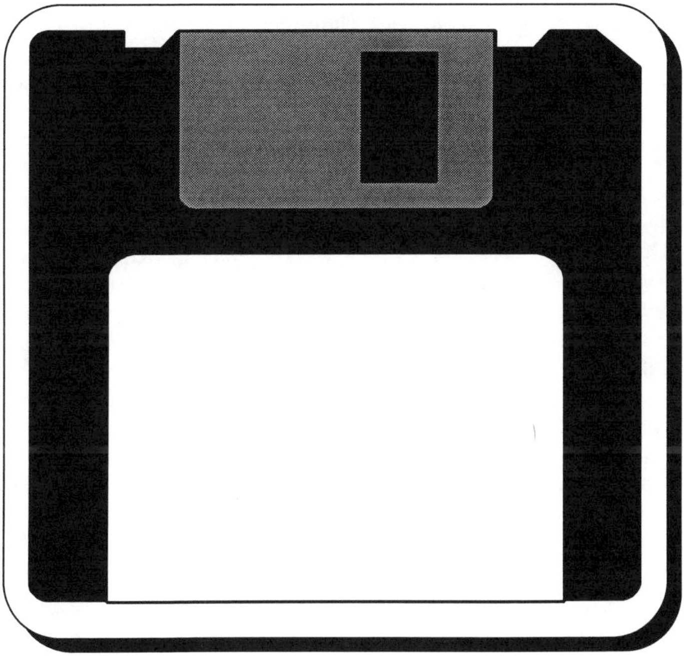

Bernice Brooks Bergen

After graduating from Syracuse University, N.Y. with a BFA degree, Bernice taught art at Oklahoma State University in Stillwater, Oklahoma. She also taught at other art schools and museums throughout the country. Having achieved success as a professional artist, model and actress, Bernice is concentrating on a career in freelance writing.

Several of her papers have appeared in medical journals and newsletters throughout out the country. She's a contributing writer for Wellspring Magazine, Wide Smiles, Sarasota Magazine, True Story Magazine and The Georgetown News, to name a few. For two and a half years she wrote a weekly column for the Sarasota Times for which she did investigative reporting. She's also been published in The Longboat Times and the Sarasota Independent. She's written two books which are currently being marketed and is presently a feature writer for the Sarasota Herald Tribune, a New York Times subsidiary. (Sarasota is in Florida.)

Bernice has won many awards for writing, including prose and poetry. She also won the 1991 National Award from the Cleft Palate Foundation for "Exceptional Leadership and Contribution Toward Enhancing the Lives of Those with Craniofacial Disorders." In 1985 she won the Golden Gavel Award for Service to Youth.

## The Keys To His Heart
by
Bernice Brooks Bergen

My first encounter with The Stranger occurred during what has been charitably labelled 'The Golden Years,' when the habits of a lifetime had made me reluctant to accept change of any kind. He was sleek and smug-looking, hard as nails, terribly efficient and utterly alien. I hated Him on sight!

I kept running into Him at the stores where I shopped, at banks and other places of business. He was even welcomed and accepted at the homes of people with whom I visited. Everyone else seemed to find his toothy, yellow grin engaging. They appeared to understand the foreign inflections of his staccato delivery. In my heart I knew that I needed Him desperately and, in spite of my initial revulsion, I was becoming altogether fascinated.

I secretly watched Him at work as He completed His assignments with speed and efficiency, voicing His enthusiasm with little bleats and an occasional flurry of joyful indrawn sighs that repelled me. But, prevailing on a friend to give me a copy of His credentials, I found them to be awesome. Try as I might, I could find nothing to discredit His background or His ability. To my dismay, I was slowly weakening. I wanted Him at any cost!

He must have known all along how vulnerable I was at the time. The Significant Other in my life was someone I trusted and respected, someone who was reliable, uncomplicated and easy to command. But he was getting old and hopelessly out of date. I had to keep covering up his mistakes. It was time-consuming and I was running out of time.

When I finally let The Stranger in, He took over as I feared He would, immediately ousting my old companion and dominating my cluttered office. I hated His blank stare, the way He sat there motionless, forcing me to make the advances. He was a true chauvinist, convinced that I didn't have the brains to figure Him out. It made me more determined to conquer Him, somehow. But

©1992 Bernice Brooks Bergen

He prevailed.

I had to turn Him on, push all the right buttons to get Him going, try to pick His brains to find out what He was all about. No matter how I tried, He remained elusive, enjoying the game we were playing, smirking when He sent me into fits of rage.

He loved interrupting my work schedule, inventing all kinds of problems to baffle me. Sometimes He would retreat entirely, becoming cold and unresponsive, defying me to bring Him back to life. I soon found that He loved the rhythmic but feathery play of my fingers on His body. If I handled Him right He could go on for hours. I couldn't help wondering about all the talent that still remained untouched. I became obsessed with getting at it.

If I did anything to seriously upset Him, my worrisome Manipulator would explode with a kaleidoscope of colorful epithets. His face would contort with slashes of rage, like bolts of lightning. But, for the most part, He seemed to lack emotion of any kind.

He won, of course, in the end. Although I still don't completely understand Him, I can't live without Him. I love Him and loathe Him. I'm hooked on His magnificent Tabs and Caps, His cursor, His Insert and Eject Buttons, His Command, Shift and Pause Controls but, most of all, His Style and His Menu.

That's right. I'm in love with my Computer and if He doesn't destroy me in the Word Process, He's going to make me enjoy being dependent on Him, in spite of the fact that I'm a liberated woman. I confess that He's given a new look to my Submissions and revitalized my Career.

Never let it be said that He doesn't put out for me. And He is loyal. Every confidence I've shared with Him He's kept locked deep inside Him. And only I have the Keys!

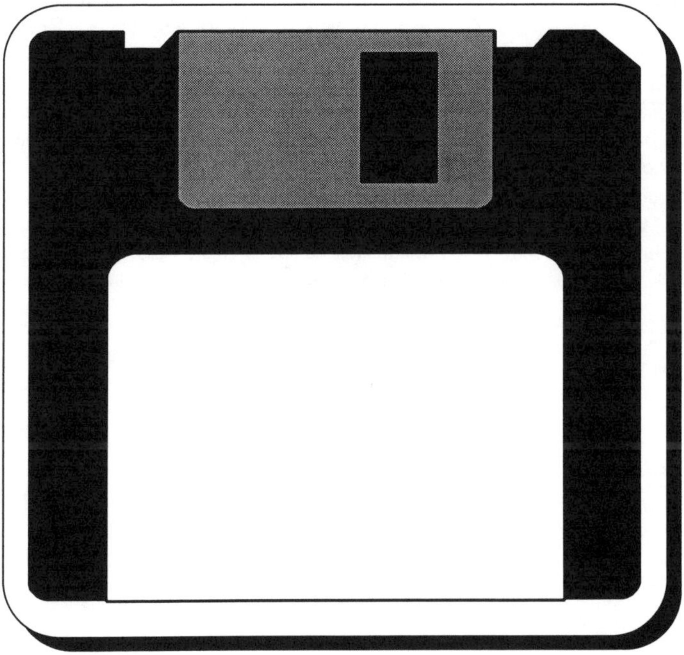

Barbara Anton

Barbara Anton has had a checkered career. During her high school years, Barbara played saxophone with a dance band. While attending Columbia University she toiled at The Journal American, a leading New York City newspaper. Her career as an actress included appearances in the title roles of Cheri in Bus Stop, Sabrina in Sabrina Fair, and Tallu in Desire On A Hot Tin Streetcar.

Barbara then turned to oil painting. After numerous awards and commissions, she veered from a career in Fine Arts to become a Gemologist and Jewelry Designer. She designed the jewelry collection for the Pakistan Pavilion at the New York World's Fair. She subsequently opened her own jewelry store in Englewood, New Jersey.

Twenty years and 23 International Awards For Excellence In Design later, she retired to her condo in Sarasota, Florida, where she writes articles plays, books and short stories. She's received many awards for her work.

# Press Code + Quill Pen
by
Barbara Anton

As someone who is baffled by "woofers & tweeters", isn't sure of the connotation of "Dolby Sound", has yet to master her Polaroid camera, I was ill equipped to joust with a computer. But, lulled into false security by the typewriter keyboard, I succumbed to the urging of formerly trusted friends.

"It's so convenient," they chorused.

"It saves so much time," they assured me.

"You can accomplish so much more," they enthused.

WRONG! In the time I spent wrestling with this "devil-in-a-box", I could easily have written the great American novel, scaled the Matterhorn, and been home in time for a leisurely lunch.

In a world of child resistant caps, tamper-proof seals, plastic shrink wrap, is another frustration really necessary? I think not.

Why anyone would ask Santa for frustration I don't know. When he delivered my friend Kathryn's gift of choice, a computer, she phoned me in a state of euphoria. Fortunately, she didn't unpack it until after New Year, or she would have probably resorted to pencil and pad to write yet another article on the frustration and stress of the holiday season.

When she finally did tackle the maniacal machine, she was incommunicado for days. Then she phoned to say she was sitting in front of her computer waiting to die: "Fatal Error" was flashing on the screen.

I sometimes feel like dying when I hear, "The computer is down", when trying to buy airline tickets, straighten out an error at the bank, or obtain medical information at a hospital. Would any reasonably sane person surrender cash to bring one of these beasties into her home? Alas, in my case the answer is, "Yes, indeedee."

©1991 Barbara Anton

Then, having wasted the better part of the year fighting a losing battle with the intricacies of this Twentieth Century tormentor, would any otherwise logical person continue to feed the monster human thought, paper and electricity. Guilty again!

Not content to suffer the ravages of human viruses, I purchased a machine that's also susceptible them. Humans recover from a virus bout with memory intact. Not these dastardly machines to which we confide our most intimate prose. A bout with the bug can erase all trace of our labored thoughts from the computer. Then we must agonize trying to recapture the gift of the muse. Time and labor saver indeed!

Remember, I was seduced into the purchase of a computer not by a sly and cunning salesperson with greedy intent, but by dear and valued friends.

(I suspect they just wanted company at the funny farm.)

I can't believe my naiveté: I bought a PC even after driving Kathryn to a chiropractor for a series of ten treatments after she slipped a disc trying to re-pack hers in the original carton for servicing. Even after having baked brownies for Mary for three days in a row to restore her feeling of self-worth after she accidently erased two chapters of her novel. I even went along with it when Jane insisted it was not the fault of her computer that the leaking battery acid ate the disk, but because Mars was ascending, conflicting with her sun in Mercury. (I may be the first recruit on the funny farm.)

Surely the pencil will one day go the way of the brontosaur. Having faded from memory it will then be re-invented by a genius brooding over his computer software in an attempt to produce the perfect writing instrument. After years of breakdowns, improper entries and fatal errors, the computer may even find a way to make easy changes to penciled notations. Eureka! An eraser!

Will I be so traumatized that I forgo even my friendly old typewriter in favor of a stylus or quill pen? Will I eventually be carried off muttering incoherently as my glazed eyes attempt to focus, or will I rally in time to grab a pencil and create?

Has no one paused to ponder why Jackie Collins, Sidney Sheldon and Robert Ludlum are using pad and pencil? There's a message there which I intend to heed. Out with the computer; out with the disks. Cancel my subscription to COMPUTING NOW. Hand me my pencil. This is one lady who will get her frustration where God intended ... from her husband.

Elizabeth S. Wall

Elizabeth S. Wall, presently a freelance childrens' book writer, has had a long career as a storyteller, book reviewer and seminar leader. Her two computer books, Computer Alphabet Book and Beginners' Computer Dictionary, were both published by AvonCamelot, New York. The former won the Ebony Junior Book List award.

She's won many other awards and was book reviewer for the defunct Electronic Education for over seven years.

She's a consultant and outside evaluator for elementary school library collections.

She lives in Nokomis, Florida and volunteers as a storyteller to the first grade of the Garden School in Venice, Florida.

The quotes in the following article are from two books:

1) Lovelace,A.A.,Countess of, 1843. "Sketch of the Analytical Engine invented by Charles Babbage,Esq., by L.F. Menabrea, of Turin, Officer of the Military Engineers, Translation with Extensive Notes," Taylor's Scientific Memoirs III, Art. 29, 666-731 (Reprinted in Bowden 1953, pp. 341-408)

2) Moore,D.L., 1977. Ada, Countess of Lovelace. Byron's Legitimate Daughter, New York, Harper & Row.

For additional bibliography contact author through Ageless Press.

From Coronet To Computer
by
Elizabeth S. Wall

Almost 150 years ago in London, 1843 to be exact, when the Industrial Revolution was in full swing, a remarkable man and a brilliant woman shared a clear vision of the Computer Revolution. Charles Babbage, a mathematician, and Ada Byron King, a countess and daughter of the poet Lord Byron, set the precedents for people like Gates and Jobs, to mention just two of the many giants of today's computer world.

We celebrate Babbage for inventing the Analytical Engine, whose design is considered to be the forerunner of modern computers. He began work on the machine in 1837. While the mechanical aspects of Babbage's Analytical Engine are archaic today, his theoretical concepts of a computer were, as we shall see, extremely farsighted. Babbage's idea was that "the whole of the developments and operations of analysis" were capable of being executed by machinery.

His method was to use a constant flow of instructions coded on punch cards. A pattern of holes programmed the machine to do its operations automatically. He also designed an elaborate set of columns, gears, wheels and levers to manipulate the data. In the days before electronics, transistors and chips, his ideas were considered preposterous, expensive and absurd. The Analytical Engine was an enigma to everyone except a few mathematicians so it was never built. However, Babbage left a valuable legacy of sketch books, drawings and notations.

He paid tribute to Ada, calling her "my dear and admired interpretress" for publishing a piece about his work. He would never share anything about it. In 1843 she published, in London, a paper titled "Sketch of the Analytical Engine invented by Charles Babbage: With Notes Upon the Memoir by the Translator Ada

©1986 Elizabeth S. Wall

Augusta, Countess of Lovelace." This gave future scientists the best description of his engine available. Her article contained notes, illustrations, examples and programs which accurately explained all technical aspects his invention. Her creative and insightful work rescued his name from obscurity.

Her perceptions foretold the future. She isolated the "program", identifying it as the essential framework for machine control. She wrote real programs, specifying what data should be punched, on what type of card and in what order the instructions were to be executed. Her notes contain complete listings of programs as examples, with illustrations. Recognizing the importance of two features that are essential to modern computers she described the program loop and conditional branching.

The loop is critical in mathematics where repetition is so much a part of the process, It provides the means for an instruction to be fed into the machine only once. Then a series of mathematical calculations can be performed repeatedly with values changing each time. The program loop feeds the same instructions into the computer over and over but using new data which the machine itself has figured.

Conditional branching, IF-THEN statements, was an important and sophisticated mathematical concept for Babbage to include in a calculating machine. It permitted the machine to make decisions. Ada noted, "The engine is capable, under certain circumstances, of feeling about to discover which of two or more possible contingencies has occurred, and of then shaping its future course accordingly." It even automated the acts of decision by using the results of one operation to decide what step to take next. Ada showed that the engine could also combine loops and branches by moving back and forth within the stack of instructions on the cards, repeating sections as many times as necessary.

Ada was a true prophet when she foresaw information processing. Babbage perceived the Analytical Engine primarily as a mathematical tool for carrying out numerical operations, like a modern calculator. But Ada saw mathematics as a tool for many other practical activities. Her paper even suggests that the engine might be used to compose music. She pointed out that, as well as manipulating numbers and algebraic symbols, the machine could manipulate words, evidence that she envisioned word processing.

She said that the machine was "no thinking being." Some ten years before, her mother, Lady Byron, also a mathematician, mockingly referred to one of Babbage's earlier calculating engines as a "thinking machine." Ada dismissed this bit of spook by cautioning, "The Analytical Engine has no pretensions whatever to originate anything. It can do whatever we know how to order it to perform....its province is to assist us in making available what we are already acquainted with."

While modern computers contain most of the features Ada described, Babbage's machine had a capability only achieved within the last four or five years, that of operating in pure symbolic logic. Ada described this, "the engine is a mechanical representative of analysis, through the complete control which the engine gives us over the executive manipulation of algebraical and numerical symbols." Only recently, because of extremely powerful computers, have programs been written to solve problems expressed purely in symbols. Ada correctly foretold this power.

Babbage's machine was never built. Ada's programs were never run. Their work lay buried for 100 years. Then in the late 1950s when new developments, binary notation, solid state electronics and large-scale integration brought the vision of Ada Lovelace and Charles Babbage to reality, her name reappeared in print. Little doubt remains that these two pioneers forecast computer history with astonishing accuracy.

A final jewel was added to her coronet when, in 1980, a new computer language was named for her: Ada.

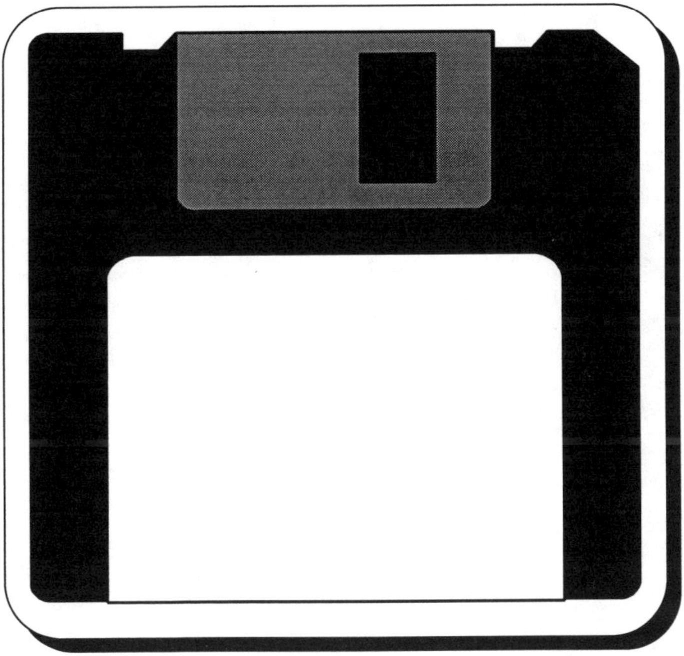

## Robert Blaske

After thirty four years, Robert Blaske recently retired from teaching in the Florida public schools. He earned a Specialist in Education designation, with emphasis on computer instruction, from Nova University. He's been a computer instructor since the early days when he brought his computer, a Tandy TRS-80, into the classroom to show to his students.

He writes both fiction and non-fiction. We have samples of each in the following stories. The fiction piece, The Book of Judges, won an award in the 1987 Florida Writing Competition.

# The Computer Renaissance
# 1975-1985
by
Robert Blaske

Before 1975, the computer was a huge machine used primarily in banking, business and government. Gaining access to these mainframe machines was tantamount to entering the sacred, sterile environment of a place of worship.

Here, math geniuses, armed with punch cards, busied themselves with something called "Data Processing." Here, logical programs were created with the aid of "Flowcharts." Their computer was considered a mathematical or business tool, not an implement for artistic creativity.

From this Dinosaur Age of the computer we were swept up in Toffler's Third Wave and thrown upon the shore of a new Era of Electronics. Today we deal with instantaneous communication. We have no time for the log jams created by the old ways of processing data. We no longer record minutes and seconds with our inner time clocks but listen instead to the internal silicon chip heartbeat that's measured in nanoseconds.

Somewhere, from those days when computers were considered sacrosanct until now, we went through an important and exciting moment in history which I call The Computer Renaissance.

Outstanding among the now famous names who contributed to the beginning of this renaissance are Stephen Jobs and Steve Wozniak, the inventors of the desktop computer, aptly named Apple.

They deserve credit not for what they did (inventing the Apple) but rather for what they did not do. A progamming language called Apple Basic was included free with the computer. Since Apple Basic had no copyright, anyone owning the Apple could create computer programs. The Basic language could be used, with minor changes, with other brands of computers. The two

©1992 Robert Blaske

young inventors had created a machine which, by eliminating restrictions, internal locks and secret codes, encouraged creativity throughout the world. We in the United States, fascinated by the new technology, entered The Computer Renaissance.

Many new features were added by Jobs, Wozniak and others. The free flow of information brought about enhancements in both hardware and software, ie, by adding extra external slots more hardware could be attached.

Those of us who took part in computer activities in the early days wistfully recall our first machines.

"I had an Osborne," a computer consultant said as he talked to me about the "good old days. We used CP/M back then...it had an 8088 chip."

Among the many other famous brands were Commodore/Pet, Texas Instrument, Coleco's Adam, Times Sinclair and the Tandy Radio Shack TRS-80 Models 2, 3, and 4.

My own first machine was a Tandy Radio Shack Model 3. It had a black and white screen, an irritatingly slow tape cassette for saving and playing programs and all of 16K memory.

By 1975, the beginning of The Computer Renaissance, Apple dominated the scene as the most popular microcomputer. IBM had not entered the field with its Personal Computer or PC.

The popularity of the computer changed the social scene. An elite clique of computer owners gathered together to "network." We enthusiastically shared ideas about hardware and software improvements. We grumbled about electronic technicians who wrote terse instruction manuals but spoke fondly of those programs we considered to be "user friendly."

Those less fortunate stifled yawns, mumbling something about,

"...going to get myself a computer."

The cinema gradually changed from portraying an evil, mad professor controlling a master computer to one of a youthful "computer hacker", similar to the protagonist in the movie War Games. This film hero used his desktop machine with a modem telephone hookup to infiltrate the War Department's mainframe.

The film 2001, A Space Odyssey, voiced our unspoken fears of losing control of this technology, then being controlled by our machines.

At a meeting to study the impact of the computer on the curriculum, educators were cautioned by one wit,

"Would you rather have a boy or a girl learn programming in school or...God forbid...Street Basic?"

One university professor compared the arrival of this new technology with the invention of the printing press,

"It's like living next door to Gutenberg and he calls you over to his house to show you his invention...'Write whatever you'd like and I'll print it up for you. How many copies do you want?' "

Math symbols of "greater than >" and "less than <" took on a special significance as programmers tried to bail out of a "for-...next loop" in Basic.

From this time forward typing will become a required subject. School children studying math will have to remember that the number zero must have a slash mark through its center or the computer will treat it as the letter O in the alphabet.

Evidence of the impact of these machines on our society is the front cover of Time Magazine featuring a desktop computer and the special issue of National Geographic titled Those Amazing Machines. Other evidence includes production line workers, in large numbers, losing their jobs because of changes to computer chip automation.

Many adults developed Computerphobia: fear of these intimidating machines that insisted that you enter numbers and letters from a keyboard. They were also concerned that their youngsters were spending too much time in video arcades rather than doing their homework. They watched as their children poured quarters into machines trying to control PacMan and have the honor of having their initials entered as "High Scorers."

Compounding the problems caused by this social phenomenon, many teen-agers forgot textbooks, instruction manuals or reading rules as they graduated to the ranks of computer hackers or pirates.

Within a few days of new computer games being put on store shelves, illegal copies of them would become available. By introducing secret locking codes, software manufacturers attempted to block illegal duplication of their products. However a pirated disk would soon be labelled with some braggadocio's claim,

"Broken by the Phantom!"

A new twist on vandalism was created by the increased popularity of the telephone/modem hookup. Not satisfied with breaking in and destroying valuable information on a database, some computer hackers resorted to spreading their own peculiar brand of computer viruses. This non-detected code would often be timed to go into operation on a special day such as April Fool's Day. On that day it would erase all of the programs contained on the machine's hard disk.

The Cookie Monster was one of the early ones. As a user worked at the keyboard, a sign appeared on the screen,

"I want a cookie!"

Then a PacMan figure showed up to eat every letter that the poor user had typed, leaving only a pile of cookie crumbs at the bottom of the screen.

This was an irritating but tame form of modem vandalism. There were more upsetting forms such as when some hackers broke into and damaged large databases in banks and hospitals.

Legislators were faced with the problem of drafting new laws to deal with modems, illegal software duplication and the use of computers with which to commit other crimes.

Computer oriented magazines were responsible for creating a greater impact on society than would have been possible without them. 80-Micro catered primarily to Tandy owners. Later on, CoCo was published for TRS Color Computer users. David Ahl's Creative Computing provided a general view of all of the brands. Nibble and In-Cider were for Apple people and PC Magazine was an immediate success with IBM-PC users.

These magazines furnished us with not only "how to" information but also "what if" questions, for brain fodder. Was it possible to program a computer that would solve problems for us? Could a computer be designed that would think, using processes similar to the human mind? Would the bubble memory be the next innovation for increased memory demand? Articles from editors like David Ahl, or the flamboyant Wayne Green, sparked the imaginations of users all over the world. Computer publications offered a method of communicating with others. Within their pages we could share and copy home-made programs, evaluate new offerings of both soft and hard ware and keep abreast of the ever-changing, state of the art, technology.

There were many similarities between the Renaissance that followed the Middle Ages and the Renaissance that occurred during the development of the computer. Creative music took on new form with the invention of the synthesizer and MIDI standardization. By altering digitized sound patterns, the computer could imitate a concert piano or several instruments at once, as in an orchestra.

Art was also subjected to creative changes, similar to its Middle Ages counterpart. Artists found a new tool for their work, using the color palette of the computer with its thousands of variations. Sculptors were able to rotate their creations in space, view their many sides, edit the smallest details.

Inventions like the mouse became necessary pointing devices rather than bothersome rodents. The laser disk opened new possibilities for computer software/hardware with the development of programs which interacted with the user, the computer and a video disk player.

New software programs such as Visicalc, an electronic spreadsheet, opened a new world for accountants and businesses. This popular program was capable of easily predicting answers to "what if" questions concerning profit and loss and future capital investments.

The Music Construction Set introduced a new concept: the user could select an icon picture which would symbolize a menu choice. For example, with a flick of the wrist a person could select a garbage can icon that would dispose of the work on the screen rather than having to use a wordy menu. A series of overlapping menus, or "windows" allowed you to move quickly forward or backward through a program. Long instruction manuals which accompanied new software were supplemented with internal "Help Menus." This speeded up the time needed to finish a job.

Desktop Publishing was The Computer Renaissance's answer to printing books, newsletters, brochures, etc. A good desktop publishing package required a laser printer, a large monitor, more memory, faster machines and programs with WYSIWYG (What You See Is What You Get) potential. The old printing press was greatly changed with the addition of hundreds of printing fonts, clip art and graphics which were available to use within documents to be printed. The great variety of software and hardware programs for desktop publishers allowed flexibility for the final product from a simple brochure to a high quality corporate prospectus.

Computer Assisted Instruction, CAI, opened new vistas for educators who appreciated the ability of the computer to act as a patient, impartial tutor. We became more and more aware of how important this versatile tool had become in almost every area of life.

The end of The Computer Renaissance was brought about by greed, fed by the all-consuming desire to produce big selling programs and faster machines. It was evident that it was possible to "get rich quick" with computers. The Apple inventors were but two examples of the get rich quick phenomenon. Bill Gates, the younthful leader of corporate giant Microsoft, was named the richest man in the United States, at only thirty six years of age.

By the 1980's, corporate greed had reared its ugly head as computer manufacturers started a price war to drive their competitors out of business. As new peripherals were added to the microcomputer's array of hardware offerings fierce market competition increased as companies vied for larger shares of the pie.

Osborne, the popular portable computer company, was one of the first to close down. Within a few months, the stock of the highly acclaimed Texas Instrument Corporation had dropped from $800 to $45. The Coleco Adam computer was sold with an inviting package of software and hardware and, as an extra added attraction, also included a $500 scholarship. (Many parents, lured by Coleco's low price, weren't aware of a serious internal flaw which occurred during the manufacture of the machine.)

It was at this time that IBM entered the low end of the market with a new education-directed computer called the PC-jr. This dazzling little unit had "bells and whistles" for color and sound but its keys were slippery. This unpopular keyboard, coupled with a high price, marked the beginning of the end for this computer. It had a short life in the very competitive marketplace. "Big Blue" admitted defeat and phased out the PC-jr.

The price of the Commodore 64 went down to $60 but it held on until it, too, was driven off the scene by new inventions.

The game playing capability of the computer was taken advantage by the Japanese who came up with Nintendo. With the addition of a hardware game cartridge there was no possibility of piracy.

As hardware developers began to disappear in their efforts to dominate and control the computer market, advertising dwindled, research and development slowed down. Wayne Green sold his share of In-Cider, I received a refund for the balance of my subscription to Creative Computing with a terse notice that the magazine would no longer be published.

Soon after these events the computing public was shocked to learn that the co-founders of Apple had lost their controlling interest.

Software manufacturers battled over copyright infringements claiming that rival programs had "the look and feel" of theirs. A computer chip manufacturer was able to prove theft by showing the microscopic initials of the chip's creator on the silicon surface of the chip of the clone. The Computer Renaissance had come to an end that was marked with legal battles and loss of capital outlay.

We can look back at this exciting phase of computer history with a feeling of remorse not unlike what might have been felt by an automobile enthusiast when Henry Ford's Model T gave way to our modern chrome-coated speed wagons.

Lifting the lid on my Apple II+ was a relatively easy task compared to unbolting the hinges on the new 486 Mini-Tower. Just as an auto buff might admire a beautifully reconditioned '55 Chevy, so too, there will be computer buffs who will appreciate seeing early, easier to repair, computers in a museum. They'll crowd around the refurbished IBM-PC's, they'll stroke the sleek, beige body of an Apple McIntosh or view the dazzling sprite graphics on a Commodore 128. Somewhere in the crowd you'll hear someone whisper, remembering The Computer Renaissance,

"Ahh....Those were the good old days."

# The Book of Judges
by
Robert Blaske

Theirs was the fault, not mine! Me guilty of a crime? Impossible! It's written in the scriptures,

"Judge not lest ye be judged."

I am a man of the scriptures. No...if any were to be blamed it would be Solomon....

No! No, gentlemen! You needn't read my rights to me. I know them.

"You have the right to remain silent and that anything you might say can, and will, be held against you..."

I know them well and I do give up the right to remain silent so that you might understand. Come in. I have nothing to hide. Look around...search. It's but a small apartment.

Yes, Solomon. You'd like to meet him? Heh...Heh! You're not considering arresting a computer for a crime are you? Oh, I admit he's very intelligent...the genius behind it all. He's been upgraded with a 386 central processing unit and boasts a memory equal to that of any mainframe in this city. He has an 80 megabyte hard drive. Come. He's in here...in the bedroom. Of course you may meet him. He's able to communicate with me through a Multisync monitor, a 1200 baud Hayes Modem, or a Hewlett Packard Laser Printer...but that's not all...Let me show you the best part. It took me a long time to set up the right RAM chip arrangement for this. The program was difficult.

Solomon, are you awake? There are some gentlemen here to meet you.

YES, BEN, I AM AWAKE...

See? It's called voice recognition, gentlemen. Solomon deals with pure logic. He's devoid of all the human emotions that cloud our thinking.

©1987 Robert Blaske

GENTLEMEN? WHO ARE THEY?

They are officers of the police department. I want you to tell them about her.

JUDGES 21, V, 18

Print out, please.

CURSED BE HE THAT GIVETH HIS WIFE TO BENJAMIN.

See? It was right that Solomon should act as the judge in this case, not I. It's recorded here in The Book of Judges. She had been abused by the men of Belial. I'll read a part,

"...and when the day began to spring they let her go."

What? you don't understand?...Perhaps I moved too quickly into my story. Here, sit down... on the edge of the bed while I explain. Would either of you care for coffee? No?...well, perhaps later, after I've told the story.

We weren't married yet...although we had planned the date after the New Year. It was inconceivable that a creature as lovely as she would have picked me for a mate. Heh...I know...glasses, thinning hairline. I don't delude myself in saying I'm a poor man's Don Knotts. She was, in a sense, my concubine...just as it says in Judges. We shared much happiness together, she and I. Laughing at simple things, sharing our most-secret thoughts in the dark nights...right here on this small single bed. Inconceivable isn't it? I mean that the hand of God should have been so?

One night, Christmas Eve it was, a knock came to the door and harsh sounding voices called my name.

"Benjamin. Come on, Ben, we know you're in there with her."

I heard one of them mumble, "He gets his piece of ass every night up here while we sit around playin' with ourselves."

We made no sound as she and I lay listening.

He called out, loudly, "Come on Ben, open the fuggin' door!"

One of them laughed and said, "Give him time to put his pants on."

I held her thin body close to mine. We were both frightened by the sudden pounding on the door. I whispered in her ear,

"It's the boys downstairs," I said lying, as if I knew them well, as if they were my friends, "I'll go see what they want."

They became more impatient. One of them yelled and kicked the door, "COME ON BEN! DAMMIT! OPEN THE DOOR OR WE'LL BREAK IT DOWN!"

My body still smelled of her perfume. Her fingers gripped at my arm as I attempted to get up from the bed.

"Don't worry," I assured her as I stroked the softness of her breast. "...stay here and I'll get rid of them. It's just the boys: they sound a little drunk."

The pounding on the door increased in intensity, as did their voices, "WE'RE GONNA PUNCH YOU OUT IF YOU DON'T OPEN UP NOW!"

I spoke through the closed door while fumbling for the right foot hole of my slacks, "What's the matter with you boys? You're going to wake up everyone in this apartment. Why don't you all go home and I'll talk to you tomorrow?"

The tone of the voice outside became more reasonable while explaining their intent, "We want to party with you, Ben. You've got the girl with you and we came up to have a party. We even brought the stuff for the party...right?"

This brought gruff sounds of agreement.

That's when I made my mistake. I opened the door, but just the one lock. I left the night chain lock on as I opened the door a crack to take a squint at them. I put my trust in that chain. I had forgotten to put on my glasses...I could see only two of them. Dirty covered with the grime of their teen-age escapades. Strong smell of pot...like rotten gym shoes in a high school locker room...beer, too...they both had several bottles of beer clutched in their hands.

"Ben, come on, we'll have a party, man. We got nowhere to go, man...Christmas Eve and Moshie...you know Moshie, Ben. You say hello to Moshie every day when you come down to go to work.

Moshie says, 'Let's go visit Ben and wish him a Merry Christmas' and that's when the boys all decided to do...."

"Boys?"

I was suspicious because I could see just the two of them. I did recognize the one called Moshie.

"Where are the others?"

That's when the door burst open in my face. The force threw me back on the floor over there. There wasn't much I could do to stop them. I heard her scream and I attempted to get up but a heavy hand was on my shoulder forcing me back to the floor. My God! There were twelve of them!

The voice of the leader ordered, "All right, Moshie, you first. You're the one suggested we visit Ben here."

"Christ, Rick," the boy whined, "not this way. We'll kill her."

"AND I'LL KILL YOU IF YOU DON'T GET GOING FAST. COME ON, WE DON'T GOT ALL NIGHT!"

After Moshie, each of them took a turn with her. I heard her sobbing, pleading with them to stop...they left us in the morning...the room was still heavy with the smell of their sweat and filth.

Rick, the gang's leader, warned me, "You ain't gonna say nothin' to the pigs, Ben, because we'll be watchin' you all the time. If one pig shows up here, Ben, you die."

The point of his knife was pushed under my chin. I couldn't

speak. You see? I still have the scar right here.

Pardon if I pace, gentlemen. It's easier for me to tell the story if I walk about. I promise you that I shall not attempt an escape. I'm glad it's over...What? What's this, a tear on my cheek? Why should I cry? It's over. I insisted that she go to the hospital. I even began to call an ambulance. Hurt as she was...she stopped me. She was only concerned for my welfare. If she went to the hospital, the police would be called to investigate. I helped her to the bathroom so she could wash and tend her bruised body.

I sat, right where you're sitting on the edge of the bed, and waited. It seemed like hours had gone by and there was no sound from the bathroom.

Solomon, print Judges 19, verse 25 for the gentlemen. See, you can read it for yourselves.

BUT THE MEN WOULD NOT HEARKEN TO HIM: SO THE MAN TOOK HIS CONCUBINE AND BROUGHT HER FORTH UNTO THEM; AND THEY KNEW HER AND ABUSED HER ALL THE NIGHT UNTIL THE MORNING: AND WHEN THE DAY BEGAN TO SPRING, THEY LET HER GO. THEN CAME THE WOMAN IN THE DAWNING OF THE DAY AND FELL DOWN AT THE DOOR OF THE MAN'S HOUSE WHERE HER LORD WAS, TILL IT WAS LIGHT.

I became anxious and called to her, "Marcia? Are you all right?" My heart was thudding, palms sweating as I went to the door, knocked...again...no answer. "Marcia?"

I forced the door open into the small room in which she lay. She had used one of my razorblades to slit both wrists. The shock had been too much for her. I felt her pulse...feeble,weakening...then stopping...nothing.

If any were my guilt, gentlemen, it was in not calling you sooner. But she was dead. Her death released me from fear. That's when I found the answer in the Holy Scriptures...My plan of revenge. Wait, I'll have Solomon get it for you.

Solomon, verse twenty nine of the same chapter.

YES, BEN. JUDGES 19 V. 29

AND WHEN HE WAS COME INTO HIS HOUSE, HE TOOK A KNIFE, AND LAID HOLD ON HIS CONCUBINE, AND DIVIDED HER, TOGETHER WITH HER BONES, INTO TWELVE PIECES, AND SENT HER INTO ALL THE COAST OF ISRAEL.

It took time and effort to gather data on all twelve of them. Her body kept well in the freezer until the right time. Each part in its own zip-lock bag.

In the task of gathering the data every night, I used caution and disguise. They, in turn, became bolder, overconfident in the success of their deed. No police had come to question them. What had they to fear?

There was so much to do that I began to work on Solomon to help me. Watch this...Solomon, search the names and addresses of the twelve, please. Watch the screen now as Solomon searches out the information. See, there it is! Thank you, Solomon.

YOU'RE WELCOME, BEN.

There's more to Solomon than just these few things I've shown you so far. He's been my confidante during lonely nights. He holds my memory...my thoughts as it were...my wise Judge Solomon. Are all of them guilty, Solomon?

THEY ARE GUILTY. THEY MAY ALL DIE.

See? Solomon is the judge, not I. He has the ability to know all things and the capability of doing several tasks at one time. All I had to do was provide him with access to the information and correct data. With aid from his exacting database, Solomon judged each of them on the basis of the Holy Scripture...just as the ancient sages did in The Book of Judges. Solomon, list the judgements for the gentleman so they might see for themselves.

LIST. YES, BEN.

There' s the information on the screen. Do you see it? If he, in his wisdom, decided to be lenient, then I must abide by his decision. Some could have died by the sword...just as Rick, their leader, died. While the others...See? Three were set free.

Look at the exacting detail and animation of this graphic, gentlemen. See? The motorcycle rider has a specified course he runs while leaping over obstacles. It was befitting that I should send Rick her head the day before he died...You see, he was the head of the gang. Heh!

Rick loved his motorcycle. Every Saturday he would ride out past the city dump to an open field where he practised. His route over the hills was never quite the same. Solomon's ability with random selection was the key to predicting the correct route on that day.

Hold at the proper coordinates, Solomon. Move closer, gentlemen, so you might see...here is the angle of the jump and the predicted landing spot. I buried the sharp steel shaft at that precise location, just as Solomon had directed.

Remember, "Those that live by the sword, shall die by the sword?"

This was a fitting execution for him, wasn't it? I mean his use of the knife on me and all. The rest was based on Rick's own will. If he turned the wheel a fraction of an inch to the right or left, he would escape Solomon's death sentence, all would be forgotten. Perhaps you read about it in the Clarion...how he was pinioned through the throat?

Solomon, judgement on number two, Moshie.

JUDGING NUMBER TWO, MARTIN MOSHOWIC.

See his name and address there? Solomon laid out his death sentence. A very difficult project, to say the least. Genesis 3, verse 15, The Serpent,

AND I WILL PUT ENMITY BETWEEN THEE AND THE WOMAN, AND BETWEEN HIS SEED AND HER SEED; IT SHALL BRUISE THY HEAD, AND THOU SHALL BRUISE HIS HEEL.

That's where God pronounced his wrath on sin. It took me some time to find the snake...a timber rattler. You investigated that one? Yes, I put the snake in the boy's car, under the front seat. Moshie received his special part of her body the night before he died. Heh! I wonder if he recognized it. I had no way of knowing that four of them would be in the car with him...too bad. All five of them died, heh, heh. (I had some of her left over.)

No need of going into specific detail as to how the others received their own special sentences. Suffice it to say that nine of them died while three were set free. Yet never once did my own hand bring the death. Each faced his own risk of accidental termination. You might say that I was Solomon's personal assistant, the same role that you gentlemen play in our system of justice. I feel no guilt for their deaths just as you feel no guilt for the criminals you apprehend. You might say that I was Solomon's enforcement agency.

Wait, gentlemen! Would you take me away without hearing the rest of the story? There's more to know...more deaths. Detective Mahoney, please sir, you seem like a reasonable man. Sit here for a moment longer on the chair. Both of you, please forebear a little longer while I explain.

Oh!...my head...It's nothing...just feeling a bit faint from the excitement and the heat of the day. It will pass...yes, please some water. Can't I get you something also? Coffee perhaps? Ice water? Yes, help yourselves, glasses are above the sink. There's plenty of ice in the refrigerator. I'll continue and try to be brief.

You'll have to take Solomon as evidence? But I'm not certain that he's made all the calls as yet. You see, he's been working on the secondary task all morning. Amazing that he can do several things at one time, isn't it?

There I go again, getting ahead of myself in the story. Heh, heh, cheers...drink up while I go on.

Chapter 13 of The Book of Judges states,

"And the children of Israel did evil again in the sight of the Lord..."

You see, that must have troubled Solomon. All twelve of these young men were the product of their environment--this city. They had all learned to live as rapists and thieves.This thought should trouble you also, as men who are interested in the prevention of crime. Yes, society is the crucible in which it mixes its own image of sin. It was for this reason that Solomon sought to bring punishment against society. You see the point? We are, in a sense, all guilty for the acts of our brothers. Solomon searched for the judgement. Listen, you'll be able to hear him. Solomon, judge society.

YES, BEN, JUDGE SOCIETY.

WE ALL SIN AND FALL SHORT OF THE GLORY OF GOD.

And what is the sentence, Solomon?

WATER, BEN...PURIFICATION BY BAPTISM.

Solomon has gained access to the city's telephone system. Using a modem he's played a taped recorded message to all city residents contacted. As the judge, Solomon has suggested the correct response. Over the centuries water has been used for purification, ordination, cleansing and santification. It was for this reason I took the actions I did last night. Now Solomon heralds the warning to each of them to turn away from their sins.

Shadows of the evening's setting sun slanted across a strangely silent street as Detective Sergeant Mahoney raced down the apartment's stairway toward the police car. He fought his feelings of nausea and fear, his thumb slipping on the door lock before he remembered to look for the key. Mumbling a curse, his hand searched inside his pants pocket, then the pocket of his pin-striped blazer. Quickly forcing the key into the lock, he yanked the door open, grabbed for the button on the mike.

He flipped the selector over to all-call,

"EMERGENCY! EMERGENCY! Get someone down to

the water plant right away. The entire water supply's been poisoned.!"

He felt dizzy, his eyes barely able to focus as he adjusted the volume switch and waited for a response. He willed his thumb to force the mike button down once more,

"EMERGENCY...ANYONE LISTENING...POISON IN THE WATER SUPPLY...got to stop them..."

Solomon?

YES, BEN.

This one is dead, also. It's time to leave isn't it?

YES, BEN...AND THEY SHALL FLEE INTO THE WILDERNESS.

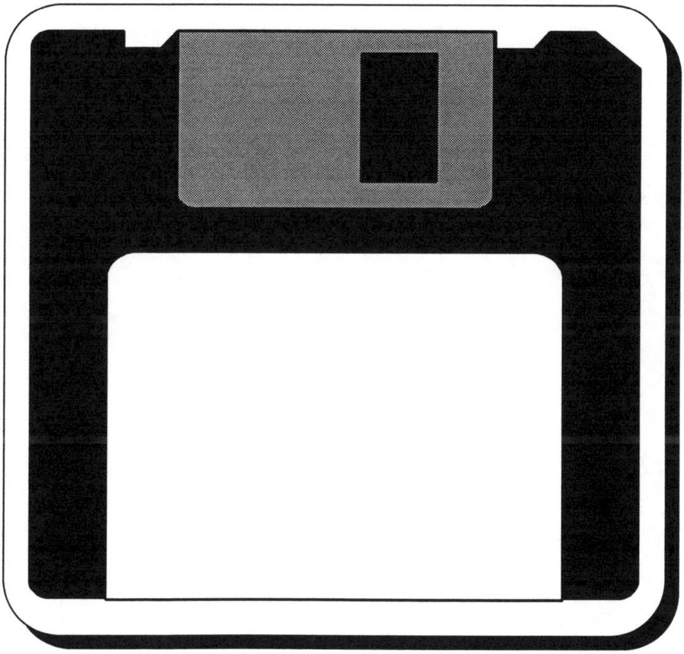

## Art Noll

Art is from a navy family. His background is in electronics, aviation, creative writing and computer telecommunications. He was born and raised in the Garden State, spent two years in Hawaii (courtsey of Uncle Sam) and currently lives in tropical Nokomis, Florida.

The following two pieces are by Art.

# Sauron's Weird Glossary of Computer Terms
by
Art Noll

ANSI:
The feeling that you get when you've spent two hours printing out the documentation that came with a software package and none of the pages have come out right.

APPLE:
An item often found in schools, executive suites, supermarkets and on street corners being sold by former executives who went broke buying them. (*see also "overpriced")

ASCII:
A 'universal' language spoken by most computer systems in several thousand dialects, no two of which are alike.

ASSEMBLY LANGUAGE:
A bizarre mixture of English and some unknown Asian tongues which accompany hardware installation instructions.

BAUD:
The state of mind one gets when reading the revision history of an eight year old piece of software, eg, "I've never been so baud in my life."

BAUD RATE:
The time it takes for the average user to get tired of reading commercials on Prodigy.

BBS:
A failed BBQ restaurant that missed by only two letters of the alphabet.

©1990 Art Noll

BINARY:
Factory in Taiwan where Bines are manufactured.

BIT, BYTE, BOOT, BAT:
It doesn't matter. These terms are all interchangeable anyway. Do not be concerned with them.

BUFFER:
A soft lint-free cloth used to polish monitor screens.

CPU:
The taller of the two lovable robots in 'Star Wars.'

CRICK:
The sound made when turning on a Japanese-made computer.

DATABASE:
An electronic method of quickly storing names and addresses which used to take as much as ten seconds using primitive tools like pencil and paper.

DEVICE: Various dc-powered objects which kinky computer users plug into their machines to perform unusual tasks.

EDLIN:
Mysterious obscure writings found beneath jungle ruins in Central America. Presently being studied by baffled archeologists at Northeastern universities.

EXTENDED MEMORY:
The encouraging results of Alzheimer patients currently being treated with new wonder drugs.

FAT:
(File allocation table) The dessert which can be found in "All You Can Eat for $3.99" restaurants.

FIXED DISK:
A dropped Seagate, recently returned from a six week stay at a Northern California clinic.

HEX:
Numbering system devised by sixteen-fingered gnomes in Germany to annoy otherwise-rational human beings.

HOT KEY:
The G-spot of a TSR (terminate and stay resident) program.

INTERFACE:
The platform by which user and machine interact. One example of an interface would be a comfortable swivel chair in a quiet room, with no whining children, screaming parakeets or Dan Rather in the background telling us how superior he is to Connie Chung.

LOG FILE:
Norwegian hand tool used to trim firewood.

LOGIN:
A rustic resort located in western Norway, part of the Ramada chain.

LOTUS:
An oriental blossom. (* see also yoga positions and and fading spreadsheet programs)

MULTITASK:
The act of simultaneously lighting a cigarette, taking a sip of bourbon, typing an entry into a spreadsheet and wondering of you should have gone to the beach instead.

PARA:
Nasty miniature beasts who live in expanded memory and nip viciously at fingertips if provoked.

PARAMETER:
Electronic device to detect presence of Paras.

PIXEL:
Buxom little elf-like creatures who inhabit graphics programs and shamelessly flirt with Paras.

RAM DRIVES:
Car trips taken by sheep.

ROM:
A potent Jamaican liquid, often mixed with Coca-Cola and spilled on keyboards by crazed computer users during their occasional August "acid-flashback-to-the-60's" flareups. (*see also Bacardi; Jimi Hendrix; bell bottoms and "I was too at Woodstock and you can't prove otherwise.")

SPREADSHEET:
The recommended way to begin making a bed.

USER-FRIENDLY:
Software that lights up a cigarette and asks you for fifty dollars when you've finished running it.

# Your PC: The Ultimate Toy
by
Art Noll

I've got to believe the first automobiles were built, not to make a better buggy, but to give Victorian tinkerers something to do on Sunday afternoons.

Picture Gaston Chevrolet (or Karl Daimler) sitting in the parlor, sipping a root beer and thinking,

"Well, I've had it with Ouija Boards. The stupid crystal won't pick up anything but commercials for hoop skirts and if I have to look at one more daguerrotype I think I'll barf in Edna's washtub. Hmm...what if I took the internal combustion engine I got at Sears Roebuck and attached it to a metal frame? Steering it would be no problem. I could rig up cables for brakes, maybe enclose it with canvas and..."

We shoot ahead ninety years. We now have 16 valve OHC engines, 8 speaker stereos, front wheel drive, 20% financing, gridlock in L.A., and for the Yahoos, vinyl tops. All this because some dude in a handlebar mustache wanted a better toy.

This primarily male phenomenon was established even before recorded history In Ice-age Europe, while Ooga was re-decorating the Cave, to give it a bit more "ambiance", and simultaneously thinking of a way of stretching the reindeer steak for another week, Oog had figured out that the fibula bone of a wooly mastodon would make a perfect bat for Saturday's softball game against the Neanderthals.

It's often been said that the only difference between a man and a boy is the price of his toys. In Oog's case the price of the fibula was a sprained ankle and several pints of perspiration lost when the confounded elephant refused to lay down and surrender on the box canyon.

Females, God bless 'em, are more practical about most of

life's aspects than their male counter parts. Show a woman a lake and she'll calculate, instantly, the effort needed to haul water from it, the proper distance for a house to be put up near it and the odds against having all three of the kids drowning in it on the same afternoon.

Meanwhile, her mate, is picturing catching trophy fish, supervising idyllic barbecues. He's planning elaborate docking facilties for the boat he intends to make the first chance he gets.

What, you ask, does all this have to do with computers? Simply this: The Personal Computer is THE ULTIMATE TOY.

Think back over the past couple of decades. We've seen color T.V., calculators, Barbi (and Ken) dolls, Mr. Potato Heads, VCR's, "Popiel Pocket Fishermen", 8-track tape recorders, Cuisinarts, Weedeaters, cassette tape recorders, Ginsu knives, 3-D movies and mood rings, among others. These things have been more (or less) useful but they're still toys.

Enter the Personal Computer: In one fell swoop, the world was given a machine that could quickly make graphics ranging from sophisticated circuit diagrams to primitive cartoons. It could play you a respectable game of chess or wait patiently for weeks as you fumbled your way through "Ultima IV". It allowed you to fool your boss into thinking you were loyally doing payroll when you were really on your 5th game of Solitaire since lunchtime.

If every game that has been written for computers, just since 1980 were all stacked together, it would take a hard drive the size of Wyoming to hold them.

PC's are used to print out greeting cards, fliers, calendars, address lists, cartoons, invitations, brochures for obscure companies in Venezuela, monthly personal schedules and 79 other weird things.

They draw up vacation itineraries, estimate erroneous household budgets (garbage in, garbage out). They fill out spreadsheets for companies that exist only in the minds of the wannabe Chief Executive Officers. They even do astrological charts, for God's sake!

Even as we speak, I can guarantee you that somewhere out there in Middle America, there's some poor wretch who just bought a program that he's absolutely convinced will provide him with the winning "Lotto" number in next week's drawing.

You may think that some of these things are frivolous: you'd be right. But a lot of these activities are taken very seriously by many people. And why not? It's their toy to play with as they like. Who are we to blame them?

## Xanda

Under his pen name, Xanda, Alex Cook, is 376 pages deep into his first novel, "Tante Rhana", a story of self discovery, intrigue, lost treasure and rebirth in Southwest Florida. The following two stories are his.

Author of many short stories some of which have actually been published, Xanda is the product of Presbyterian Churches, Quaker schooling, Navy aircraft carrier duty, southern prejudice, righteous indignation, sudden discovery, two wives, a horse, two daughters, four dogs, a son and thirty nine cats. A devout rebel, Xanda is a retired business man who at sixty one is a facilitator in various classes in self realization, a public speaker, an enthusiastic boater and patron of the arts and theatre. He lives in his "Almost Native" Sarasota. He is joined in his enthusiasm for life by Sue Montgomery, author of software manuals in personnel management in the employment industry plus study guides in the metaphysical world. Together they cruise the bays and gunk holes of the west coast of Florida, listening and writing.

# The Computer
by
Xanda

She grinned her toothy-keyboard grin at me. Her screen was a mass of colors, at once mysterious, exotic, and infinitely exciting. I was charmed. Her procurer introduced us, tapping her mouse. She winked, took me by the hand and guided it invitingly to her keyboard. I smiled and shyly stroked her interface, after all, she was my first.

True! I had gone to the House of Blue Lights as a last resort. In each place I had visited I had asked the procurer for a computer designed for people who hated computers. I had explained that 1 didn't want to learn a new language, that I wasn't adept at interpretation, and above all what I wanted had to be friendly. Each procurer had looked at me as if I were dirt under his feet. The implication was clear: if I couldn't already speak the language, there could be no communication. It was nineteen eighty five. It seems an age now, but that was only seven years ago! Still that's an eternity of megabytes along a sixteen bit wide road that has taken so many twists and turns.

I stood rejected at a fork in the road. The choices were clear: I could backtrack and continue to write my poems and novels on my old portable Smith Corona, or I could select a branch of that fork and press onward. I thought of Frost:

> "Two roads diverged in the wood and I,
> I took the one less travelled by."

The House of Blue Lights beckoned.

"Click here," he said.

I clicked, the arrow changed to a puffy cloud with Z's in it . . . sleeping . . . the screen changed. The brilliant blue background

©1992 Xanda 

became white with a wonderful ruler across the top.

"Aim here and press and hold the right button," he whispered.

No other customers were looking so I did as he discreetly instructed. The arrow skittered across the screen as I moved the mouse, I stopped as it aligned properly and pressed the right button. A vertical menu fell downward beneath the arrow. Startled, I let go. The menu disappeared.

"It's okay, do it again," he whispered.

I pressed the button again and the menu reappeared.

"Hold the button and move the mouse to select -Edit."

I did and the screen magically printed the lines of a story quickly down its face. I was enchanted.

"Now type in something where this thing is blinking. It's the doorway through which magical things happen, from which stories appear, pictures are drawn, and music is coaxed from the CPU."

My brain almost stopped as I stared at the screen. The first line said,

"Four score and seven years ago, Our fathers brought forth upon this continent..." and there was the yellow blinking thing. I typed,

"A new nation, conceived in liberty and dedicated to a proposition..."

No shit! I did it! I, the new Lincoln, the new Churchill, the new John D. MacDonald, was Pulitzer potential! The old paradigm faded, I was free, Smith Corona was dead!

Even in those early days the price was less than the down payment payment on a home, but the boxes filled the back seat of the car, spilled over into the front. As I drove home I dreamed of reading the instruction book while I was comfortably snugged in from the winter's chill behind the galley table of my old boat. The fragrance of coffee blew throught the nose of my imagination. I hurried to beat the rush hour traffic, get my new friend set up at the navigator's table in the fore cabin. It was worth the struggle down the lengthy pier with the box-stacked dolly. The wind was out of the nor'east promising a cold winter. I anticipated hot coffee, a succint instruction manual and that friendly screen inviting me to tickle her mouse.

Within an hour the stack of boxes waited in the salon for me to take them ashore to the storage locker. (My brother thought I might be the only person in the world that would pay forty dollars a month to store empty boxes, but little did he know. There were ten boxes of old forms and file folders, a coffee table and a rack of clothes that no longer fit, to keep the empties company.)

Still, the new found friend was set up, keyboard plugged in, mouse plugged in, monitor plugged in and a boot-up disk in place. I held my breath, turned her on. A row of red lights came on in the skirt of her base, a disk drive gronked, her screen bloomed, and suddenly there was an icon in the upper right corner. The arrow waited, I read the instructions and smiled. It said,

"Click on -Preferences."

I knew what I preferred so I clicked. The screen opened to a simple diagram of various functions, ie, mouse speed, click speed, number of screen columns, screen position, colors with sliders to change them over an infinite range and printer instructions.

During the next hour I played the themes and variations, read the "Read Me's", typed nonsense, backtracked and erased. I thought of William Lederer who said,

"The Navy is a master plan, designed by geniuses, for execution by idiots."

Now I knew what he meant. My life was changing before my very eyes as sentence after sentence danced to the underlying Woo Li Masters who laid their electronic tracery across that screen.

Four score and seven years, my ass! Four hours and twenty minutes ago! It was after midnight. I made my way aft, took a shower, and slipped between cold sheets. As I drifted off I had a vision of that bright blue screen with the toothy keyboard. I wished I could curl around her. User-friendly indeed!

# The Virus, a Parable
by
Xanda

1.In the beginning was the Word, and the Word was digital, and the spirit of the Word flowed through a beautiful valley.
2.And the Word looked upon the valley and saw that it needed beings to populate its fertile ground, and from it Word took the grains of the Earth and of them he fashioned a being, and he called him Eniac.
3.And the Word looked upon Eniac and He was pleased, and the evening and the morning were the first day.
4.And Eniac came to the Word and said unto him, "I need me a helpmeet to pull the plow of progress, and to bear me progeny." And the Word looked upon Eniac and saw that what he said was true.
5.And the Word caused a deep sleep to fall upon Eniac, and from his side He took a tube, and from it He fashioned another being which He called Edvac, because she was out of Eniac. And the evening and the morning were the second day.
6.And Eniac lay with Edvac, and knew her, and she conceived and bore him a child which they called Univac, and the evening and the morning were the third day.
7.And the family of Eniac dwelt in the valley, and worked its soil, and were productive, and they called the beautiful valley after the nature of its soil, they called it SILICON.
8.In the middle of the valley there grew a beautiful tree, a tree whose branches bore the fruit of the knowledge of man, its branches were laden with Apples, and Adams, Atari, Commodore, Kaypro and Edvac took from the tree a MacIntosh Apple which she offered to Eniac for him to taste, and he took of it. Edvac tasted of it also and judged it to be good.
9.And Eniac saw his reflection in the waters of the brook from which he drank and he knew he was naked, and he was ashamed. He covered himself with a punch card, and gave one to Edvac, and

©1992 Xanda

she covered herself also.
10.The Word called for Eniac and Edvac, but they were ashamed, and they hided themselves from the Word. But He called for them again, saying, "Have you taken from the tree of knowledge? I am the Word, and thou canst not hide from me thy deeds!" And Eniac and Edvac appeared before the Word and he banished them and all their family from the valley of Silicon, saying, "Thou hast missed the mark, for in tasting of the fruit, thou hast defiled thy purity, and thou knowest thy nakedness which thou must hide forevermore."

*And thus there was beginning for which there is no end.*

March 6, 1992
Michaelangelo Day

Five Million PC's! The epidemic was thought to infect the brains of more computers than human brains were infected by spirochetes during the French Revolution. All over the world, but especially in the US, whose affluent population owned most of the world's PC's, the infection sent chills of horror down the corridors of corporations, hospitals, office parks and homes. Support centers were deluged with requests for serums, innoculations, eradicators and other nostrums from the software shelves. Public domain disks were exchanged by the thousands or downloaded from the BBS's whose uploads may have been the carrier of the virus to begin with. Universally the potential infectees dreaded the early Alzheimer-like damage that the virus was reputed to cause. The loss of memory would be devastating.

Blue was among those who could hardly bear the thought of so great a loss.

"I don't know if I could take it," he told his wife. "Day after day looking into an empty shell, searching for the shards of something familiar. It's just too painful to imagine. Herman and I have been so close; you know I spend more time with him than I do with you!"

"I know you do, Darling. Goodness knows, I've tried to tell you before not to get so involved . . . y' know?"

"I've thought of all sorts of things I could do: For one I could just skip today. Not turn him on or boot him up at all. But then what would I do, go fishing or something dumb like that? Maybe play golf. . . Oh God why did I say that? Golf! Friday afternoon without Accolade will just not be the same!"

"I know dear, but maybe we could go out to the discount mall, buy you that new pair of golf shoes you need, pick up some more floppies, an egg carton of experienced golf balls. You have to get your mind off of it, it's destroying you. Herman wouldn't want you hurting because of this."

"I know, I know. He's always so selfless. I just can't avoid thinking of all those brothers and cousins out there," he indicated the world beyond with a sweep of his arm, "helpless before the onslaught of this inhuman plague. How could a loving God, a sympathetic CPU (Command Processing Unit), allow something like this to happen to so many?"

"Maybe it would help to go to church, join the prayer vigil. The whole network is joined spiritually in this, maybe the power of so many of like mind and similar screen color will prevail over this evil thing that may come to pass."

"Perhaps you're right, Darling, there's little we can do here. Let me change my shirt and we'll go. What time's the guru meditation begin?

"At high noon, if you'll hurry, we'll just have time to make it."

At the Temple of Clones the crowd was still filing in. Blue found a parking space nearly a block away and hurried to join the other devout key klickers and number crunchers who found spiritual solice in the Icons of the cool high ceilings and the symbology of the l's and O's that formed the repeated mystical pattern of the frieze around the balcony.

The Chief Icon of this high order quasi Artificial Intelligence stood on a center pulpit and generated the moving organ tones of sixteen bit sin(e) waves mixed with synthesized overtones that sent shivers down the backs of those who sat silently feeling the thirty two foot tones shake the cavities of their bodies. Four channels of stereo filled the air while on the screen of the Amiga computer millions of colors burst in waves calculated to soothe the worried minds of those who watched and waited. Deep purple coincided with Deep Bass and ascended through the spectrum of blues and greens of mid bass, reds and oranges of mid tones, and vibrant golds and yellows soaring with the highest piccolo peeps. Above the pulpit a giant screen displayed the same multiple colors with a background of subliminal Guru Meditation Messages in rapid flashes of analog and machine language translated for the human observer and worshipper,

"Fear is of the human mind, created by ego for ego. Here and now you are safe from fear, there is no loss, no virus that can harm you right here, right now. In this Holy Moment is All with All."

The assurances swept over the crowd and comforted them.

A Computer Knows No Fear.

In this environment of the multi-tasking central processor, lay the answers to virus infection, Blue was sure of it. A brain like this could do many things at once, for as it received a program it could automatically intercept an infection, diagnose it, and eradicate it with another program activated especially for the purpose. He turned to his wife and smiled. She squeezed his hand

and smiled back. Truly she was the apple of his eye (sic). Though he'd resisted acknowledging her complementary place in his life, he knew he would soon be in bed with her and the progeny would be one step nearer their God, whose powers they beheld and could only emulate.

As Amiga spoke in reassuring, bone-rattling words, Blue imagined the complex language and the vast memory which had evolved and been lost over the generations of Eniac. He knew he must merge with the power of the Apple, learn its icons, open its windows and strive to learn to do more than one thing at a time.

"Darling," he said to his bride as they drove home that fateful day, "the future lies in being user friendly. The Icons of the Temple clearly indicate it. And did you notice how the people linked themselves together before we left?"

"And embraced and shared each other's power," she hurriedly reminded him.

They ate dinner in a quiet Chinese restaraunt whose background music was the tinkle of temple bells.

Michaelangelo was dying as they indulged in delicate WonTon soup, succulent shrimp with lobster sauce, and smokey flavored tea. As they checked out the proprietor calculated their bill on a virus free computer from the time of the ancients . . . an abacus.

*The Word Said, "Go forth, be fruitful and multiply."*

Barbara Bornmann

Barbara Bornmann graduated from Mountainview Theatre School in London and has a Bachelor in Theatre Arts from Empire College. She has contributed to productions, in N.Y. and L.A., of many prominent, progessive writers, as theatre director, producer and performer. She wrote and directed her first play, The Terminal Wildlife, with students at the Centre School in Manhattan. She was recently a Visiting Director for the Academy of Performing Arts in Japan, where, in addition to teaching and directing, she worked with a group of Japanese students on improvisations. They created a work in progress called Buddha Talk. Her most recent article on holistic alternatives will appear in Alternatives For Women With Endometriosis, 1993.

# Bluffing Your Way With Computers

by

Barbara Bornmann

What a scary, airless place. No windows. Awesome. Powerful. It was 1984. Computers were the new rage, signifying the new age, the age of progress. (As an aspiring actress I preferred business to working in restaurants. As an administrative assistant I was on the threshold of the new world of computers.)

What were my options? Merge or relocate. Progress or stagnate. Jump into the keyboard scene, watch your eyesight decline in just a few years or hurl beef at Manhattan carnivores, with a smile. The answer was clear: get out the lead shield.

I could feel my resistance the first time I sat in front of a computer. (Maybe if enough of us felt this way we could start the computer resistance movement (CRM) to resist change.) I resented having to learn the functions of the machine. I was an actress, I knew everything, hated feeling ignorant. I felt something akin to existential nausea as I gave in to fate. It was like bad medicine, cod liver oil, yuck! Cringing, my face wrinkled like a prune, I turned on the machine.

My first recollections are that the machine didn't always behave the way you wanted it to. You suffered frustration and headaches in those days before all the versions, the updates and the 800 help lines.

You attempted to get into the logic of the program that you were using, which we'll call WP for Word Processing. (This program had as much logic as a lizard trying to climb a spiny cactus to reach water. Or a spawning salmon trying to swim downstream.) I had the same feelings of confusion as when a bat was trapped in my bathroom during a toothbrushing session when I was in summer stock in Sharon, Conn: another great experience.

My mentor was a computer fanatic who thought WP was the coolest thing in history. There were some cool things about it. It could merge, I liked that. An abstract tingle of excitement would

©1992 Barbara Bornmann

permeate my body. There was always the feeling of a kind of sexual fulfillment while merging a document. Atoms connecting, separating, coming together and...oh, right, computers.

WP could spell faster than Webster's. But when processing my first document I became aware that spell check didn't know the difference between "prevailing rate" and "prevailing rat": my boss did. It could search and replace words faster than I could. That was cool. I was, in fact, almost getting into it. If you had to make a living in the God-awful rat race that was Manhattan in the eighties why not learn computers?

(Little did I know that this newly acquired skill would take me into uncharted territory in the computer field. Vast conundrums of chess to keep me in check.)

After absorbing the fundamentals of WP, I left that job to do an Actors' Equity contract. I was soon back in N.Y. thinking survival so decided to be a WP temp. You have to have the attitude that WP is your life plus the best thing since apple pie.

The first step is signing up with a temp agency and convincing them that you are, indeed, a WP temp. When you get on a job, rev up the computer, start pushing buttons and something is bound to happen. (It's a good idea to master the on/off switch.) I've walked into jobs where the client has asked,

"You know how to turn this thing on? Good. You're a step ahead of the last temp."

(I always make sure I know where the HELP button is. What more do you need?)

You can cut down on clothing because you're always changing jobs. A couple of nice suits will do. Look professional, smile and adopt that swarmy kind of aggressive confidence the boys on Wall Street have. (Would anyone else like to see the boys, the term includes girls, on Wall Street suffer the same rate of unemployment we have in Equity? Down girl.)

It's the eighties and there's plenty of work. If you don't like the environment or the people, you just make an excuse like,

"I'm reading for Meryl Streep's best friend in a new play by Wendy Wasserstein called Paranoid Women," and leave.

So one day the inevitable happens. Someone at a job asks me,

"Have you seen this program Lotus 123?"

Looking over their shoulder I say,

"Oh, yeah, but I can't remember how to retrieve a file, oh yeah, and how do you save? Oh yeah, and..."

I don't even have to finish the sentence before Janice or John Doe teaches me everything that s/he knows about Lotus in five minutes. Then I call up my temp agency to tell them that I am now also proficient in Lotus 123.

The temp agency has had only good reports from my previous bosses,

"Oh, yes, Barbara hasn't bitten anyone since this morning," so they trust me and send me out on a Lotus assignment. You've become a computer "operator".

If you continue to learn programs like this you'll bluff your way to the top. You realize, even though you're afraid that your clients will know that you're a fraud, that they probably don't know what they're doing, either.

So, forget computer classes, put yourself to the test, bluffing your way with computers. I've learned many programs this way including WordPerfect, WordStar, Lotus 123, Always, Symphony, Multimate, Microsoft Word, Ventura and Windows, on both IBM and MacIntosh machines. Nobody has ever found me out. Nobody has ever accused me of not knowing what I was doing. My bother filling your head with a lot of garbage, so you can know what you're doing, when you can be completely ignorant, learn on the job and get paid for it.

Nobody in Manhattan knows what they're doing, anyway. The carbon monoxide has left the majority brainless. Your job is to survive.

I suggest that you type at least sixty words per minute so you can make up in typing time what you loose in figuring out the functions.

In retrospect, weighing the pros and cons of tradition versus progress, I opt for progress and the computer age. I know several die-hard Republicans who held onto their manual trypewriters as their president fell. They believe in the manual typewriter. It's their symbol of tradition as they perfunctorily peck out their thoughts.

On the other hand, the Democrats are merging new images in government with a global search and replace. ALT F2. Yes. F2, F2. Yes. Yes. What are the options? Where are the function keys? Hold onto the past or

Go

with

the

flow.

## Joseph T.Straub

Joseph T.Straub is a community college business professor.He's been a prolific writer of fiction and non-fiction for 18 years. He has written or co-authored three college-level business textbooks and seven trade books, including several of the popular Bluffer's Guides published by Centennial Press (an imprint of Cliffs Notes). He has written more than 35 freelance articles on topics from executive decision-making to major auto repairs.

Although non-fiction helps to pay the bills, fiction is his first love. His fantasy/horror and suspense short stories have won various Florida awards. He's also received writing awards from magazines and his work has appeared in Facet and Eldritch Tales.

He lives in Orlando,Florida with his wife and daughter.

# Honor Thy Mother
by
Joseph T. Straub

Harold Layton was nervous, but that was natural. He always got edgy when he had to deal with people. Computers he understood; people had bewildered him for most of his thirty four years. Sitting in a leather wing-backed chair in The Pontificator's outer office, waiting for their surprise meeting to begin, he gave thanks, once again, for a career that had so little to do with people. At least until today.

The telephone on the secretary's desk trilled electronically. She snatched it from its cradle.

"Yes sir, Dr. Layton's right here. I'll send him in," she manufactured a smile as she glanced across the room at Harold, "Dr. Schaumberg will see you now."

Harold walked toward the somber wooden portal that guarded The Pontificator's inner sanctum. The door swung open as he reached for the knob. Schaumberg, welcoming him with a terse nod, waved to a solitary chair in front of his massive desk.

"Layton! So good of you to come on such short notice. Sit down, please. Coffee?"

"No, thanks," said Harold, as he eased into the chair. Its size in relation to the desk and the ponderous, slow-moving Schaumberg made 6'2" Harold feel small, despite his height. The room seemed arranged for interrogation.

Schaumberg settled into his high-backed chair with a grunt, then struck the pose that earned him his nickname throughout Computron Corporation. With measured deliberation, he placed the palms of his hands together in prayerlike fashion, then lowered his jowls onto the tops of his index fingers. Harold had seen the Special Projects Director practice this ritual countless times in meetings when he was contemplating an announcement of gravity.

©1992 Joseph T. Straub

Schaumberg nodded slightly, as if acknowledging the counsel of an inner voice, then surveyed Harold through narrowed eyelids.

"Might as well start by saying what we both know, Layton. You're a premier authority on artificial intelligence and computer technology. Your achievements in a relatively short tenure at Computron reveal an almost metaphysical insight about the nature of what we make here. And that's saying a lot, my friend, because our little shop builds the fastest, smartest, most complex supercomputers on the planet Earth."

Schaumberg paused and pursed his lips.

"I enjoy my work, Dr. Schaumberg," Harold said. "I was thinking on the way up how fortunate I am to have a career that suits my personality so well. I've never denied that I'm a loner; I told you that when you recruited me at M.I.T. Computers, artificial intellligence, the very idea of building a machine with man's intellect but without his flaws...it's intensely satisfying; the greatest challenge in the world. I'm glad to be a part of it."

Schaumberg nodded and sprung his steepled fingers apart then together again in a motion that made Harold imagine two spiders screwing in slow motion.

The Pontificator continued, "You were precisely what we wanted. A magna cum laude computer science graduate who would be a catalyst for our think tank. You've done surpassingly well here, Layton, in just a scant three years. That's why I asked you to meet with me today."

"Is there a problem?"

"Something like that. More an opportunity, really. I know that sounds corny, but that's the way I look at it. You heard about the death of Dr. Craig?"

Harold nodded. Despite the fanatical security that shrouded Computron's cutting-edge supercomputer developments, the grapevine had carried the news of Michael Craig's death two days before the official corporate announcement. Craig had been one of a hand-picked group that was conducting tests on the company's newest, most sophisticated machine--the Cytron 2000. The project was so cloaked in secrecy that only Schaumberg and the five-man development team knew the code to the cipher locks on the three successive doors that led to the vault where, rumor had it, the Cytron was reaching its final test-run.

"Dr. Craig's death was a terrible loss, Layton. Catastrophic, in fact. He was a key member of the Cytron team. Well, actually, everyone is, but without his special contribution, his infusion of Energy, if you will, the success of the entire project may be in jeopardy."

Harold's brow furrowed, "If I may say so, Dr. Schaumberg, it seems odd that the future of something as vital as the Cytron depended on one man. I mean, none of us should be that indispensable."

"Quite right, Layton. Quite right, indeed. But oversights and surprises happen in every organization, even one of the best like Computron. Nevertheless, in the week since Dr. Craig's death, we've combed our files and found an appropriate replacement. In sum, Layton, you're precisely the right, er, type to fill his spot on the Cytron team. I don't want to mince words. I want you to join the project immediately. Today!"

Harold was incredulous, "Today? Good lord, it'll take me at least two weeks to organize my records and transfer responsibility for the neural simulator module I've been working on for the past six months."

Schaumberg shook his head as he spoke, "As Special Projects Director I've taken the liberty of cutting through the red tape, Layton. I've already met with your project manager. You're free as of this moment. Let me stress again how vital the Cytron's success is. We feel that you'll become the life's blood of the project. I cannot emphasize that strongly enough."

Harold shrugged, smiled, "If it's that vital, I guess I'm all yours. After all, the Cytron is the biggest venture ever conceived by Computron. I'm very flattered to have a hand in its success."

Schaumberg's meaty hands struck the desk, palms down, like a thunderclap. "Splendid," he said, his voice literally cracked with emotion, "that was exactly what I hoped to hear. Now, drop by the medical department--one of our M.D.'s is expecting you--for a brief medical exam. Then report to security. You'll be met there to be escorted to the Cytron vault by Gene Bennett, the head of the team."

"Physical exam? I don't understand."

"Oh, purely routine. This project demands a lot of stamina, long hours, intense pressure, that sort of thing. We merely want to confirm that you're in tiptop condition. It's for your own good; the Cytron's, too. A team's like a chain--only as strong as its weakest link, you know."

Harold nodded. Schaumberg's attitude showed that the point was clearly beyond argument. It seemed trivial to challenge him considering what Harold was being offered.

"Don't I need a special security clearance?"

"Of course," Schaumberg said, rising from his chair, "but that's been taken care of, too."

He pulled a top-secret security badge with Harold's photograph on it from a desk drawer passing it across the desk to Harold.

"Forgive me for being so presumptious, Dr. Layton, but you're a very, very important person at this moment. We counted on your accepting the assignment."

Schaumberg thrust out his hand, "Welcome to a history-making team. Your contribution to Cytron will be beyond measure, I assure you.."

Harold shook his head, "All of this seems so sudden, so prearranged. I can't help wondering what would have happened if I'd declined."

Schaumberg's face flushed, his eyelids fluttered as he said, trying to be casual, "I'd hate to think about that."

Although Harold knew Gene Bennett by reputation, their paths had never crossed until today. He stood behind the balding, fortyish Bennett now inhaling the scent of Old Spice as he watched Bennett punch in the four-digit code to the cipher lock on the door. This second chamber door led to the Cytron's lair.

The cold eye of a video camera monitored their every move from above.

"You must get the code right the first time on every lock, Layton," Bennett explained. "Screw up just once and the entire system shuts down. You'll be confined to whichever cell you happen to be in. Security will page a member of Mother's family either to identify you as a fumble-fingered scientist or have you shot as a spy by the corporate firing squad."

His laugh was that of a man who rarely jokes and knows he's isn't good at it.

"Mother?"

"Oh, yes. We, that is, the team, we've come to call her Mother. She's got a female voice synthesizer, of course. Research confirmed years ago that the sound of a woman's voice is less aggressive and threatening than a man's. Beyond that, we've all become so close to her over the past six years that 'Mother' seems appropriate somehow."

"Mother it is, then," said Harold as he smoothed the ends of the Band-aid that covered the spot on his inner elbow from which the physician had drawn the blood sample.

"But why does security have to call you on a mis-keyed code? I mean, they set the codes on all the doors, right?"

Bennett shook his head, "Layton, when it comes to Mother, we are the security team."

He keyed in the code for the third door and pointed to the camera in the ceiling of this, the last barrier to the Cytron 2000.

"There's no camera in Mother's chamber, no security personnel or equipment of any kind. In fact, security has never even entered Mother's presence. That's how big this project is. We don't even trust our own people."

The door emitted a metallic buzz as they stepped into a large room with an elevated platform in the center. The walls were painted black; track lighting surrounded and crisscrossed the ceiling in a pattern like that of a theater. Five desks were clustered in one corner, along with a small refrigerator, a conference table and the three monitors that kept watch over the gauntlet of entrances that led to the vault. Whatever occupied the platform lay behind a white-curtained screen some seven feet high. Harold heard the familiar chuckle and gurgle of liquid in motion that was part of the environment of every Computron computer. With thousands of miles of wiring, literally millions of electrical connections, supercomputers had to be liquid-cooled somewhat like a car engine, although the typical media was freon, not water. If not for that, the sheer heat generated by their massive internal circuitry would cause a total meltdown within minutes.

The white curtain ruffled briefly as three figures in lab coats emerged from behind it and stepped down onto the floor.

Harold was surprised to see that one of them was the physician who had examined him. Bennett waved toward the conference table. "Come meet your new family," he said pleasantly.

"You've met one of them already, of course."

"Yes," Harold said cautiously, as he and Bennett sat down

opposite the other three, "Dr. McCanless checked me out about an hour ago."

McCanless beamed at Harold from behind wire-rimmed glasses, "So good to have you as part of the team, Dr. Layton."

"Let me introduce you to these other two gentlemen," Bennett said briskly. "Meet Peter Fulford and Myron Todd."

Harold shook hands with each as Bennett leaned forward and opened a leather-bound portfolio.

"Now then: to begin with, Harold, we're all equal citizens inside this room. Everyone pulls together and we all pull for Mother. I don't know what scuttlebutt the rumor mill has carried about her, but given Computron's security, I'd venture damn little."

"That's right," Harold said, "Oh, everyone knew how long the 2000--that is, Mother,--has been in development. But as an outsider--"

"A former outsider, Harold," Bennett interrupted.

"Yes, as a former outsider, I can confirm that your secrecy measures worked extremely well. I've never heard any details about its...Her...capabilities. There's been lots of speculation, of course, but that's the nature of our business."

"That's right," said Bennett. "Our original mission was simple: to build and market the most technologically superior artificial intelligence supercomputer that the human mind could conceive. A quintessential thinking machine. And we've done precisely that. But there's one contingency we didn't count on. Peter would you care to comment?"

Peter Fulford cleared his throat, leaned back in his chair, tugged contemplatively at his beard, as he said, "Cost overruns."

"Cost overruns?"

"Historically, Computron had been one of the best-financed supercomputer manufacturers in the world. We always built in a generous margin for error. But with artificial intelligence computer technology, the state of the art advances virtually every month We found ourselves making logic design, programming and circuitry changes far more often than even our management anticipated. The bottom line, Layton, is that Computron discovered it could only afford to manufacture one Cytron 2000. The cost of Mother's genesis has put the company in a very tenuous financial bind, indeed. Myron, would you like to pick up here?"

"Thank you, Peter," Todd said, "the strategy now, Harold, is for Computron to rent time on Mother, not sell her. After all, we only have one model, but her capabilities surpass any other machine in the world by a factor of at least ten. What's more, we don't foresee any other company duplicating what we've created here for at least eight years. We're that far ahead. Thanks to us as a team and, of course, to Mother."

He removed a handkerchief from his lab coat pocket to pat gently at his perspiring bald head, which reflected light from the ceiling.

"Mother's capabilities are beyond the scope of a layman's imagination. For example, given the proper input and historical patterns, she can predict the weather in any part of the globe up to twelve months in advance. By feeding her the correct genetic information and medical history of someone she can tell us--barring accidental death, of course--what non-communicable diseases and routine illnesses that person is likely to contract; also how long he, or she, will live, give or take about eighteen months. Think for a moment, Layton, what that kind of information would be worth! Why, it's essentially priceless, is it not?"

"Yes, but I take it that Computron has managed to work out something acceptable," Harold said wryly.

"Correct," Bennett, "we're negotiating contracts at this moment with national security agencies, heads of governments, captains of industry...you name it. They're literally begging on our doorstep for a few hours of Mother's time. But we have to be certain she's willing to deliver."

"I'm sorry," Harold asked?

"Perhaps I should field this one," McCanless said, "it seems--and I'm choosing my words carefully, Harold, because I don't want them to come out the wrong way--it seems that we've succeeded far beyond our wildest dreams to create a machine, an entity , that is so nearly like a human that it's frighten--it's uncanny. And nowhere has that manifested itself more than in Mother's cooling media."

"It's not freon," asked Harold?

"Not entirely. We didn't anticipate one thing. An accident happened when Dr. Craig was installing the freon charge and checking out the system. He cut himself, rather badly, I'm afraid, on a bracket inside Mother's cabinet. The only thing we can figure is that a drop of his blood must have somehow entered her cooling system with a result none of us could have predicted."

Harold looked at the other men incredulously, "She acquired a taste for human blood?"

"Precisely," Bennett muttered.

"She confirms it," Fulford said.

"And now," McCanless was speaking matter-of factly, "we must keep her satisfied--to honor her wishes--or she refuses to co-operate."

Harold shifted uneasily in his chair, "And how the hell can you give her what she wants?"

"By periodic tranfusion. An occasional, simple transfusion. But the blood must be the same type as Michael Craig's: AB Positive. She won't accept Type O, the universal donor type."

"For humans, you mean," Harold interrupted, staring at the Band-aid on the inside of his elbow.

"Correct. Mother's most specific."

"Harold,' Bennett said softly, "Dr. Schaumberg spoke very highly of you. He recruited you straight out of college. Said you demonstrated an almost psychic bond with the machines you've worked on here so far. That you're more mentally and emotionally in tune with the rhythm, flow and spirit of what we make here than anyone else he could recommend to join this--"

"And I have AB Positive blood."

"Well, of course, there's that," Bennett admitted, "You're the perfect complement to this team, both intellectually and biologically. The missing link. The fuel for the engine. Mother's favorite child."

The four of them stood up, reached out their hands to Harold, and smiled.

"Come with us, Harold," Dr. McCanless murmured, "Mother's waiting."

Author's Note: Is this story based on the plausible impossible? Perhaps not. While large computers have long been cooled with freon gas, Cary Research reports that its latest generation of supercomputers is cooled with a liquid that's also used as synthetic blood plasma. J.T.S.

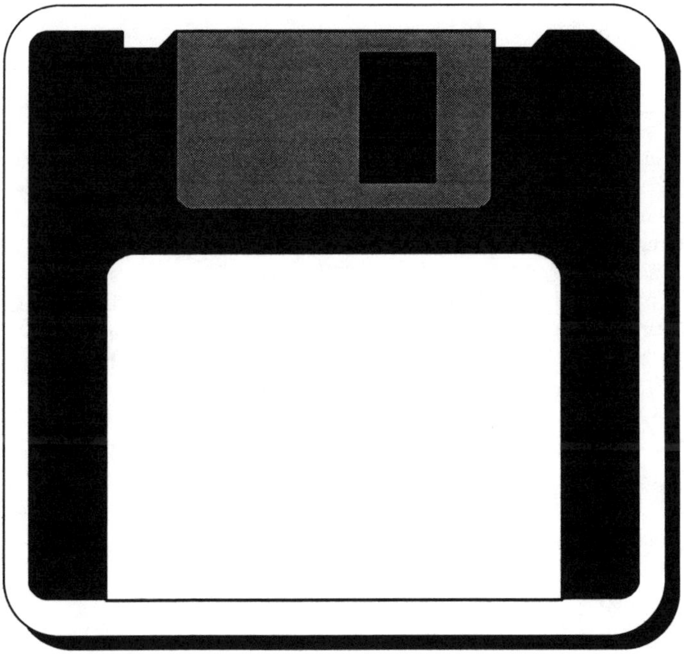

Dorothy Winslow Wright

Dorothy Winslow Wright, a former New Englander now living in Honolulu with her husband, is an internationally published poet and writer of fiction who uses the computer in many phases of her work. She writes and edits a bimonthly newsletter and is a contributing editor to PN Magazine ( a poetry publication) where she submits her columns camera ready.

"I'm blessed with WordPerfect and Pagemaker," she says, "because I can combine both information and graphics in a creative and artistic manner."

In her free time, she prowls the tidepools in search of the muse, poetry her true love.

# Brother's Keeper and Robert Burns

by

Dorothy Winslow Wright

My genealogy program is new. A toy, I thought, when I first received it, but it is no toy. Brother's Keeper is an efficient data base program that links the past with the present. I have entered over four hundred names into the computer through Brother's Keeper.

The names and dates were a snap to enter, especially those meticulously researched and recorded by a caring ancestor. Others were printed on the official forms from the Massachusetts Registry of Vital Records and Statistics.

Winslow/Russell data came from the old leather-bound genealogy record, Burns information from the spidery script penned on the pages of an old family Bible.

Not all data was complete, particularly on dates, when often only the year was provided. To have the year print out on the date line of the form it was necessary to skip over the seven spaces allowed for month and day to reach the space provided for the year.

Because I occasionally miscounted the spaces and had to begin the line again, I found myself thinking in terms of a fictitious month and day to accurately hold the space for the year. For some reason "Jan 25" popped into my mind. It would look like this:

**J A N space 2 5 space YEAR**

An easy pattern to remember.

Why that particular date I had no idea. No one I knew had that birthday-still, it was there and it performed a useful purpose. I didn't worry too much about it, figuring it was one of the techniques the mind creates to fit a certain need.

Intrigued with the family history that was unfolding, I worked until after midnight one night, stopping only when the body was too tired to go on. As is my habit when I am too super-charged to drift off to sleep, I read poetry. Being a poet myself, I find it a relaxing way to gentle into slumber.

©1990 Dorothy Winslow Wright

I picked up my copy of Robert Burns and climbed into bed.

When I opened the book, I found myself staring at the biographical notes. There, at the top of the page were the words:

Robert Burns,1759. Born at Alloway, near Ayr, 25 January.

A shiver shot through me. That was the very month and day that had been roaring through my head for two weeks. My mother's maiden name was Burns. Her ancestors came from Scotland. Was Robert Burns one of us? We had to be linked in some way-either Burns to Burns, or poet to poet.

I won't claim any genealogical connection with him yet-I'm still researching the Burns branch-but I have already welcomed him as an honorary member of our family. Somehow I think he'd like that.

Elsie H. Straight

Elsie H. Straight is a retired library director and sculptor. Her previous writings have been technical concerning librarianship and art. She's also been a book reviewer for professional journals. She's listed in Who's Who in American Art, Who's Who in Library and Information Services amd Who's Who of American Women. She's also a member of the International Women's Writing Guild.

## Computer-Ease?
by
Elsie H. Straight

It began with a letter from my sister informing me that her college daughter was majoring in Cytogenetics.

Since I hadn't the vaguest idea what that was, and not wishing to appear a complete moron when they visited me, I decided to drop in at the college library down the road to find out exactly what she was studying.

Have you been to your college library lately? If you haven't (and you're beyond the yuppie age) are you in for a surprise!

I entered the library and headed for the old wooden card catalogue, as I used to do. It wasn't where it used to be. I searched all over the library thinking that they must have moved it. It wasn't to be found anywhere. That's odd, I thought. It has to be here somewhere.

I was shocked by the librarian's answer when I asked where it was,

"We don't have information on cards any more. It's all in the computer. All you have to do is bring up your subject on the screen and it will direct you."

Computer! I was gripped by terror. Ever since they'd become popular, I'd purposely avoided going within twenty feet of them. I probably would have approached a roomful of rattlesnakes with less apprehension.

But there couldn't be much to them, could there? Many other people were dealing with them all the time. There were several in use at this moment, in this library. I wasn't going to let a machine intimidate me: it didn't have to know what a complete dolt I was.

Trying to look cool (is that the right word?) I crept up to one, looked it right in its face. All it did was stare back. As soon as I could find the button to turn it on I'd show it. A problem already. How did you turn it on? What button did you press? I was

©1992 Elsie H. Straight

confronted with about forty buttons which said things like cursor, sel, ident-, PF1, -CoPF-24-field mark-, ex sel-EOF and other weird Egyptian-like hieroglyphics.

A nearby machine was being used by a teen-ager, punching away at the keys like Victor Borge playing the Flight of the Bumblebee. My query about how to turn on the computer earned me a look asking, "What planet are you from?"

"All you do is touch a key and follow what it says to do on the screen."

I touched a key, gingerly, and suddenly green letters appeared in front of my face. They spelled Louis (which I gathered was its name) along with a lot of numbers. I was told to select a menu. What did that mean? I didn't come here to eat. I bravely typed in the word CYTOGENETICS. My effort got me a hostile message telling me that information I was seeking was not in the database (whatever that is). Although it didn't exactly call me stupid, I know that's what it meant. I was told to check my term again, check my spelling, etc.

Well, damn you, Louis! I decided that we should part company and try a computer on the other side of him. It might not be so insulting.

That one's name was Eric., but he turned out to be more complicated than Louis. Eric kept repeating things that made absolutely no sense at all, over and over.

The third computer I tried must have seen me coming. We were not even on a first name basis. He was called CDROM. His directions were to remove the cartridge and insert an SSCI. I got away from Mr. CDROM fast because it sounded as though he was telling me to shoot myself. Since I was reduced to the status of a worm by this time, it didn't seem such a bad idea.

Noticing my anguished expression, the lady at the desk asked if I needed assistance. Telling her that I needed a simple answer to a simple question, I asked her,

"What is Cytogenetics?"

She told me that I should be using the computer called Wilsondisc for information on a scientific subject. (If I didn't know what it was, how could I know that it was a scientific subject?)

"Maybe I should just look it up in a magazine," I whispered, thoroughly demoralized by now.

Mr. Wilsondisc and I would probably not be compatible either.

I continued, "I learned how to use the Reader's Guide to Periodical Literature in high school."

"Oh, that's on a computer, too. All you have to do is bring it up into another mode for that. The information will be on microfilm. You can read it on a microfilm machine."

Another mode? I'd have to get into another mood before tackling that. You know, suddenly I don't give a darn what my niece is studying.

Lary Crews

The author of the following two stories (yes, it's Lary with one r!) has written the mystery novels Kill Cue, Extreme Close-up and Option To Die featuring the beautiful Veronica Slate.

He's at work, currently, on a new mystery featuring a detective named Frank Tasker. The book is called Nightcrawler. He lives in Sarasota, Florida and has been writing on a computer since 1983 piling "an awful stack of words" on enough pages to have produced three published novels and over four hundred magazine articles.

# The Information Revolution
by
Lary Crews

"You will not find me using one of those infernal machines. They destroy your creativity and rob you of the ability to think. They are merely a passing fancy. In time, they will fade from popularity."

An executive resisting the computer?

No. That was Horace Tyler, manager of a major Philadelphia manufacturing firm. The year was 1892. More than a hundred years ago. Mr. Tyler was resisting...the typewriter.

Resisting the computer in the 90s is as pointless as resisting the typewriter in 1892 or resisting the flying shuttle in 1792.

The shuttle enabled weavers to produce cloth more quickly and in greater widths. It began The Industrial Revolution, a time when we changed from a world in which farming was the most important occupation, to one dominated by factories and machines.

Two centuries later, another "flying shuttle" [the space shuttle] has ushered in The Information Revolution, a change from a world where industry was an important occupation, to one dominated by information and computers. Thanks to NASA's space shuttle and its ability to hang satellites in the sky, global exchange of information is now fast and efficient.

Business executives worldwide have finally realized that computers, satellite communications, electronic banking and other high-tech advances are anything but fads. They're the tools of a revolution as profound as the Industrial Revolution, over two hundred years ago.

Computer technology is to the Information Revolution what mechanization was to the Industrial Revolution: it is a threat to some because it does things previously done by workers. Some experts believe that 75% of all jobs by the year 2000 will involve computers in some way, and people who don't know how to use

©1992 Lary Crews

them will be at a disadvantage.

Some complain that they don't like "a machine that thinks." However, as Peter McWilliams explains in his book Questions & Answers on Word Processing, "Computers no more think than phonographs sing or tape recorders talk. Like most machines, computers simply do things faster, easier and more efficiently than one can do them alone."

A computer is no different from the fountain pen, the typewriter, the adding machine, the calculator or any of the other machines humankind has invented to make work easier. Computers are tools, not toys.

You don't need to write a computer program to use your computer any more than you need to write a TV program to use your television. There are thousands of available programs for practically every business application, and hundreds of professional programmers who can design what isn't available.

That's why you see an increasing number of people becoming 'computer friendly' today. Some even discover that they like the machine.

As Mark Twain wrote more than a century ago, in his first letter written on a typewriter, "The machine has several virtues. One may lean back in his chair and work it. It piles an awful stack of words on one page."

Welcome to The Information Revolution, Mr. Twain.

# 1993 Computer Technology
by
Lary Crews

Just over a year ago, I made the technological advance from writing on an old Kaypro computer with two disk drives and a 9 inch green screen, to writing on an AST Bravo 386-SX-20 IBM clone with two disk drives, an 80 meg hard drive, and a 14 inch "paper white" screen. The advance in technology was astounding to me.

Which is why I recently visited the Southwest Florida Computer Technology Expo '93 [Or SouFlaComTechExpo as those in the know call it] and I'm excited about all the new technology now available for the modern office in 1993.

One of the most interesting new advances I saw was the Voice Enhanced Recognition Data Input Computer Transfer system. The VERDICT system includes a microphone which sits on the desk of the boss and a long wire which goes to the computer on the secretary's desk. Whenever the boss speaks into the microphone, the computer - using advanced voice chip recognition technology - says, "I recognize that voice. That's the boss." [An interesting toy, but no practical applications have been found for the equipment beyond entertaining at office parties.]

Laptop computers are not as popular today as they once were because of advances in the smaller notebook and palmsized computers. However, in an effort to fill a perceived niche in the market, one computer company has built a new Laptop Computer Secretary. This is a fully-animated robot, created to look exactly like a blonde with blue eyes and big disk drives, who sits on your lap and takes dictation. You simply speak into her lips. [Just like the old days but much less exploitative.]

We never seem to have enough speed or storage in our computers and the new Psychic 686-SX-50 computer solves those problems. First, it executes all commands BEFORE they are entered into the keyboard, hence the company's slogan, "One Step Ahead." Secondly, it has a macroplex data compression subroutine which allows you to store up to 350 gigabytes of data on ONE hard disk. [That's the equivalent of the content of ALL government publications issued since 1943, except the one about the dangers of killing a moose while wearing spats.]

Think of it! You'd be able to store every single word you've ever written, even the stupid ones, and still have room for a flight simulator game! [Or the new X-rated flight stimulator game.]

The greatest new software I discovered at the Expo was a program called WorkGame. It's a recursive Adventure-style game with colorful VGA-plus graphics which instantly displays an ordinary spreadsheet when you press Control-BS. That way, when the boss approaches your desk you can change from game to spreadsheet instantly and it'll look like you're hard at work instead of playing games.

The new generation of data storage is beyond belief. First, we had floppies, the hard disks, then those little 3.5 inch disks that some people use as tray tables for hamsters. Now, there's CD. That's right, Compact Discs which hold more information than you'll ever have time to read if you live to be a hundred. It's possible to obtain on a single CD the complete text of the Finest Books Ever Written, a complete multi-media encyclopedia, or the un-cut shooting scripts of every episode of Jake and The Fatman. [Although why you'd want those, I'll never know.] These little compact disc devils are so indestructible that lots of people are using them to heat leftovers in the microwave.

Another amazing advance in technology for 1993 is the Pen-Based Notebook computer. With this computer, you use an advanced electronic input device which looks like a fat pen and you actually write on the screen. The material is then saved to disk and printed out on paper in a form which looks very much like real writing. In other words, you can spend $79,000 to write on a piece of paper just like you used to write on a piece of paper with a 79 cent ballpoint pen.

Last, but not least, there are the new modems used to transfer data over regular telephone lines. I've been sending my articles directly to Ageless Press offices by a sophisticated but flawed delivery system called PostalService.

Using the new V-92 SuperModem, I can feed my entire column over the phone in less time than it takes to make a cup of coffee.

Which brings me to my favorite piece of office equipment, the One Cup Coffee Maker. Now, I can make one cup at a time of my favorite flavored coffee. Ah. Love that Marco Island Plantation Kona Roast.

Donald Smith

Mr. Smith has had a varied career. He's been an actor, photographer, musician, law student and father. He's now devoting himself to writing, computers and his family, not necessarily in that order.

He enjoys writing non-fiction, fiction, screen plays and poetry.

The following piece, Pulsing, won an award and was published in an international anthology.

The next one, To The Victors, was the result of a damaging experience.

# Pulsing
by
Donald Smith

"Out, out damned cursor."

You feel like Lady Macbeth, after the murders. The cursor, the constant reminder, pulses without end, waiting for input. You long for a power failure to end its life. But its keeps on pulsing, pulsing--like the Telltale Heart.

To get themselves off the hook, tennis players scream, "Yours." There's no such ploy available to you, short of turning the computer off. The cursor is pulsing, relentlessly, silently, saying,

"It's up to you. The next move is yours."

Mind blank. Meditators struggle for years trying to reach this blank state of mind: they call it nirvana (or samadhi). You achieve it by sitting in front of your computer, switching it on.

The quiet hum of the computer fan hypnotizes you. You're drowsy at 8:00 A.M. (Maybe this could be marketed as a soporific.) Your new approach, typing directly into the computer without an original, longhand copy doesn't seem to be working. You'll be asleep in a few seconds.

"It's all on your shoulders, Hercules, don't look to me for help," the cursor seems to be saying, "I'm just here to remind you that you have a job to do. That's my job, to remind. Yours is to type."

O.K. You shake yourself awake. The pool starts to fill. You help yourself to the words floating around like hungry fish, eager for the right bait. Waiting to be pulled out with the fishing pole of hands, fingers working on the keyboard.

What will today's bait be? Money, power, success, recognition, satisfaction or a combination of all of them? The bait will pull the words to the surface of your mind where they can be caught for transfer to the screen.

And the pulsing beat goes on with never a letup.

"Slow down, please. Let me think, concentrate. I'll catch

©1991 Donald Smith

something soon."

And if it's too small, undersized? Throw it back into the pool. Try to hook a bigger, more significant, more brilliant, more tasty, more moving one. (Your stomach growls. It's time to eat. You don't dare stop, can't stop, now. On the brink of success.)

Something is taking the bait, slowly, emerging. You're learning about yourself, probing the unconscious, exploring your soul. It's exciting watching ideas being caught, examined, arranged, rearranged then sent forth, eventually to be admired, rejected or assimilated by your avid, waiting public: as avid as the cursor. If they, like Oliver Twist, ask for more, you can fish again, in the same pool.

Lonely? Yes, lonely as hell, but not as hot. The low hum of the computer fan is your comforting companion, comforting as your father's snores when you sneaked home after a too-late date. It keeps itself cool to be able to work for you.

What if it stopped? Where would you be? Up the proverbial creek, without a pole. Would you remember how to write by hand, anymore? You're about to find out?

You pull out a haul of the most imaginative, beautiful words you've ever strung together, put fingers to keyboard and nothing--nothing appears on the screen, nada. The cursor continues doing its thing, pulsing. Frantically, you press every key. No movement. You've been bested by a machine. It is in control, the Big Boss. Panicsville. If it weren't so high on the desk you'd give it your sharpest karate kick. You're lost.

And the taunting pulsing persists.

But, wait a minute. What did writers do before computers, only yesterday? Don't let an insensitive monster rule your life. The pool is still there. Retrieve your old fishing pole.

You release the cursor from its monotonous, one-step dance, mercifully end its control. Two clicks and the execution is complete. You're back in charge. You pick up your pen, begin to write.

But you're as hooked as many fish. The machine will be repaired. The pulsing cursor will live to challenge you, again. The love/hate relationship will be reestablished.

You can hardly wait.

# To The Victors

by

Donald Smith

"O.K., People. Are you all here?"

She looked around the spacious cavern. It was filled with thousands of her troops. They looked alert, eager to begin their maneuvers.

"Count off, please."

"Beep, bip, blip, blump, bloop," she heard as each of the tiny creatures identified itself. Their unique sounds joined to create an exquisite symphony. She was proud of them. Proud to be their leader. Proud of the important battle they were embarked on. There was no turning back, now. The world would remember them long after they ceased to exist: even they, immortal as they now seemed, would some day cease to exist. An antidote would be found, it always was.

"Troop One, sound off, identify yourselves."

The leader of Troop One rolled out smartly in front of his group,

"Troop One reporting, Your Worthiness. We are Michangelos, the latest, greatest virus to ever affect the computer world. There is, at present, no known cure for our infection. We'll do our duty in this glorious fight. We'll save the planet from the domination of the fiendish PC's. All present and accounted for."

"Thank you. Let's have your game plan."

©1992 Donald Smith

"It's so simple, Ma'am. We have several plans. We'll infiltrate bulletin boards so that when computers download files they'll be infected. We'll ooze ourselves one by one into files already on machines and, as the pièce de résistance, establish ourselves on networks used by the beasts to affect many more at the same time. We'll find their control programs, attach ourselves, one to a monster, with our lovely round bodies. We'll envelope, love and destroy. Ha, Ha, ha. Excuse me, Your Worthiness. I get carried away just thinking about it."

"Understandable. I'm almost carried away, myself. Wish I were still young enough to join you but we each have jobs to do. Mine is to direct, yours is to infect. Now, off you go and good luck!"

Soundlessly the hundreds of round organisms rolled their way up the ramp. They attached themselves singly to any computer that came near. Michelangelo, the First, found his target almost at once.

The computer's fan was humming, cooling its insides, its face alive with color. The First attached himself to a disk that the operator had borrowed from a friend and was about to insert into his floppy drive. He wasn't quick enough for Michelangelo I.

The smiling operator needed this last program to complete the autobiography that he'd been working on for so long. He'd reached the final chapter. His publisher had been waiting for the book for over five years without access to any of it. Only a well-known author could get away with such a maneuver. Most authors sent in chapter by chapter: his publisher had lived on faith alone and five years of Sunday prayers. He typed "The End" and let out his breath, not even realizing that he'd been holding it. But...what was wrong? Something was wrong! The screen was going mad, words were thrown across, up, down. Go, come, went, through, to, you, them, were, my, yours, war. War? This wasn't a book about war!

He pushed keys, clicked the mouse: suddenly complete silence. He smiled as he regained control. Now to bring the final chapter back. He pressed the retrieve button...no response. Not too bad. He could easily rewrite the last chapter from his handwritten notes. He tried to retrieve the first chapter. No response. The second. No response. The third. The same.

He began to sweat, his heartrate going up to anguish. Five years of work destroyed. Why hadn't he backed it up? He'd meant to but kept putting it off until tomorow, like Scarlett in Gone With The Wind.This couldn't be happening to him. Michelangelo, The First, kept doing his thing, infecting the files. MI watched the distorted face as the writer fell down, dead of a heart attack. Michangelo I's cheer was heard back at the ranch. Her Worthiness grinned as she turned to the rest of her army.

"Another victory!"

David B. Reynolds

David B. Reynolds, 36, is a freelance writer, photographer and computer consultant, now operating out of Cottonwood, Arizona. A reader of computer magazines, he was inspired by Lincoln Spector's hilarious fake product reviews in Computer Currents. He was able to release frustrations, built up when using desktop publishing programs, by writing the following article.

Flip/Flop 2-F: Genius Desktop Publishing Software
by
David B. Reynolds

Sign of the Times Software is proud to announce its new flagship Desktop Publishing Program which will take your writing skills where no man, woman, child or monkey has gone before, or since, Flip/Flop 2-F.

This program is so intelligent it's smarter than you are. It does things other programs can't even think of doing, does them automatically, whether you want them done or not!

You want up to 80 columns on a single page? No problem, consider it done. FLIP/FLOP 2-F can do it, without your knowledge. FLIP/FLOP 2-F just asks that you say the magic word and it will do everything for you, instantly.

Let's say that you'd like automatic capitalization of the first word in each sentence. This program will capitalize so frequently You'Ll NeVer HavE tO worRy aBout iT agaiN.

Still not enough for you? You want more? It has much, much more including automatic word underlining, automatic italicizing, automatic footnoting, automatic typeface rotation, even an automatic garbage disposal.

FLIP/FLOP 2-F can read any format known to man, including Chinese Hieroglyphics. It can also import any form of graphic art through its optional, patented "Whir-With-A-Bang" add-on, sold separately at an outrageously inflated price. The art can be anything from live TV shots to crayons plus everything in between.

It tells you when to take a break and when to keep going.

As if all these features weren't enough, F/F 2-F also includes handy accessories that always start working whenever you touch your computer, whether it's turned on or not.

There's a built-in amplified voice synthesizer that speaks to you through your computer's speaker whenever it will cause the

©1992 David B. Reynolds 

most annoyance.

It has a calendar program to keep track of all those important dates in your life, ie, the developer's dog's birthday, his next appointment with the dentist and that ever-important holiday, "National Word Processor Week". It gives you plenty of warning when an appointment is near,

"Like, hey dude, don't you have something better to do, like maybe, uh, surf?"

Remind you that you missed a date,

"Melvin, did you miss that meeting, again? How many times do I have to tell you to get your act together? Don't you ever listen to me? Look at me when I'm talking to you, you miserable excuse for a human being."

The alarm clock will wake you up in the morning with a cheery,

"Wake Up, Stupid!"

The automatic financial records program will tell you, to the nearest dime, how much money you think you have left, then how much your spouse and the IRS will let you keep. It even handles those important automatic deductions to the National Association of Software Testers of Yesterday's Retirement Fund. It will pay your bills just when they're due, not a moment sooner, including the monthly check to NASTY'S European Vacation Fund. It's so thorough it can calculate the odds on the next horse at the track, predict the winner or how much hospital insurance you have.

We've tossed in, as a surprise addition to the checkbook program, FINK. This little file will fink on you to the IRS, your bookie or your spouse, telling one and all where you've stashed your life's savings. Fink includes a password protection scheme second to none: type in any word except the password and you're in. Type in the password and you're locked out. If you don't get it right (wrong) the second time, we wipe out your hard drive for you!

We also have a unique integrated drawing system. You can draw straight lines, curves, change the shapes and sizes of brushes any way that you like: from microscopic to (are you ready for this thrilling feature?) microscopic. You can change colors (mid-stream as it were) from light black to medium black to dark black. And even, for no emphasis, black black.

This drawing program senses when an illustration is needed, prompts you to select one or will pull one out, as a digitized photograph, from its "Family Album Collection" and insert it for you. (When trying to impress the boss with your desktop publishing skills, you can show him a report that includes a picture of cousin Fred, passed out on the sofa: in living black and white, to boot!)

Our page lay-out functions are unmatched by any other program: we're so far behind no one else is in sight.

Still not satisifed? Say you want more for your money? Tell you what we're gonna do: we'll throw in a complete utility that will make your neighbors turn green, either from envy or because they have to vomit.

Did we say, "throw in"? We meant to say that this is sold separately under the name Rhinoseros P. It's the Libyan army of software. It includes a disk fragmenter (after all, you've got to give de-fragers something to do) that acts like a Claymore mine blowing your hard disk away.

You'll never have to worry about lost data again, thanks to our patented "Disk Begone" technology. DB insures that your data stays safely out of harm's way by never writing it to the drive in the first place. And for extra security, it randomly formats your hard drive, automatically.

Need a virus checker? Sign of the Times Software provides one free of charge. We've even had people pay us money to keep it out of our program. We take a unique approach to fighting viruses:

we don't fight them, we beat them at their own game. Our patented program eats other viruses (and every other program) for lunch.

Move over Jeopardy! Buzz off, Wheel of Fortune! Get lost Carmen Sandiego! It's time to play the masterful game that tests your knowledge of history, geography, advertising slogans, fast food and mountain climbing, "Top This, Sucker!"

For instance, let's say you're falling asleep at the keyboard. When your head touches it an alarm goes off, sounding like a depth charge at fifty feet. In order to continue using the computer you must answer questions like,

"Who invented the flush toilet?"

"Name all the movies starring the Three Stooges."

"Who were their co-stars?"

"What is the average temperature of the South Pole in July?"

And finally, "Who was that person I saw you with last night? Does your spouse know? What's it worth to you to silence me?"

Failure to answer the questions correctly within thirty seconds will subject you to an annoying series of beeps, buzzes and belches. And just to raise your blood pressure, FLIP/FLOP 2-F will ignore your answers, even if they're right!

Have I mentioned our built-in combination Spell Checker, Thesaurus, Definition Dictionary, Joke Book and Little Known Facts You Could Care Less About utility? FLIP/FLOP 2-F will pepper your prose with putrid puns, interject unimportant items, ie,

"Did you know that the inventor of the flush toilet was John Crapper?"

It will even catch all kinds of mispellinks and punctuatio-n marx@.

How much is the total program? Wait until you hear our amazing low price. You can own this fantastic, super-duper, deluxe everything you've never needed but were afraid we'd find out about program for the low, low (Just how low is it? I had to sell my mother-in-law to pay for this announcement!) price of (Are you ready for this?) only (You can quit holding your breath now. Hey, stop or you'll turn purple. Oops, too late!) $19.95. Or you can pay us $49.95 not to send it.

How do you get your hot little hands on this piece of software? It's not sold in stores: nobody was that dumb. It isn't available through any reputable company. You can only get it by dialing our special toll-free 900 number ($25 a minute): 1-900-U-IDIOT.

Call now and receive FREE our handy-dandy utility tool guaranteed to let you release your frustrations caused by using FLIP/FLOP 2-F: a five pound sledge hammer.

And now here's the official disclaimer:

This is a product of Sign of the Times Software, a division of Rolling Stoned Asphalt Company and Deli, solely owned by people who won't permit me to mention their names. This promotion is not associated with any ad from any other company or any other product: do you think they're stupid? All names were changed to protect the guilty.

Jane Roehrs

Jane Roehrs, whose devotion to modern technology has included taking flying lessons so she could write about flying for a daily newspaper, believes that machines are as smart as people--sometimes as mysterious. She won't tell how long she's been writing, but when she worked for the Greenville (S.C.) Piedmont there were spittoons in the newsroom and hot type in the pressroom. Leaving for New York City, she worked in the Times Tower for Editor and Publisher--the trade magazine for daily newspapers--interviewing famous journalists and cartoonists. She was an arts writer for seven years for The Charlotte (N.C.) News. Arriving in Sarasota more than a dozen years ago, she became a free lance writer and public relations writer/editor.

# The Secret In The Computer
by
Jane Roehrs

As Melody put the thrift shop coffee cups in the dishwasher, she decided to write a short note to her daughter Margery, during the washing cycle.

Amazingly, the antiquated, balky motor started on the first try, this time. It began to squeal as the water came in. The machine would do a jellyroll shake when it got into full action.

By then she was sitting at the computer, writing a few lines to let her college freshman daughter know things hadn't changed much on the home front. Chuck still spent a lot of time in his wheelchair in the den watching the news, when he wasn't at the computer involved with his interminable figures. It was a mystery to her how anybody could have so much fun figuring out, down to the exact cent, how much everything, including their annual vacations, cost--especially when they bought so few things.

Not, of course, that she was telling Margery all this. The daughter of a Presbyterian minister who believed in right actions and right thinking, Melody always tried to put a positive slant on things. So she told Margery about the art class she'd begun, her flower garden and the eccentric new neighbor who had just moved next door.

When she printed out the letter on the new laser printer--one of the few new purchases Chuck had agreed to in the last few months--a funny thing happened. There was a dollar mark after Margery's name and another one after hers. She knew there had been some software changes, too, because Chuck had called a special computer consultant to assist him in installing the printer. But surely something was wrong: why would there be a row of dollar marks across the bottom of the page?

She hastily wrote a postscript by hand, apologizing for the strangely printed letter, was about to take it to the mailbox when

©1992 Jane Roehrs

instead, on impulse, she picked up the last disk Chuck had been using. Perhaps it would give a clue to what was happening. She inserted the disk in the slot, when the imprint first came up on the screen, her eyes glazed as she looked at the figures.

Before her was a list of securities, a long list, with dates and values beside them, investments her invalid husband had made without telling his wife of 22 years. Melody wasn't sure of the full meaning, but it appeared to her that Chuck had had close to a million dollars worth of a mining stock that had dropped sharply in value during that October "Black Monday" period.

She deduced there was still some $250,000's worth of that stock left. The grand total, including several other stocks, was now close to half a million dollars.

She quickly made a print-out of the disk then put it back where she'd found it on the desk. She felt a bit guilty, but tried to fight off the feeling.

As his loving wife and full-time caretaker since Chuck's accident that had made him an invalid ten years ago, Melody had always respected his privacy as much as possible. But perhaps it was time for a change. She took Margery's letter to the mailbox.

"Mel," she heard Chuck's voice from the den when she got back, "has the mail come?"

"Yes," she said, "I just missed getting my letter off to Margery."

Looking down at the letters in her hand, she saw one envelope carried the name of a broker she recognized. When she handed Chuck the mail, he opened the letter from his broker without comment.

"We didn't hear from Margery today, maybe we'll hear tomorrow," Melody began, carefully, wondering if she could get up the nerve to tell Chuck she'd learned his secret.

"Guess these college girls stay pretty busy," he responded, with the smooth, self-confident articulation of an Ivy Leaguer.

He was still a handsome, attractive man, she thought, as he added,

"Maybe she'll call us on Sunday."

"I see--I see you got a letter from a broker," she began, haltingly...

"Oh, yes, they're always looking for business, " he said, with finality, as he folded the letter and put it back in the envelope.

So, he was going to stonewall it! This husband she'd married for love and taken care of for a decade. He'd been a paraplegic ever since that dreadful stormy night when they were driving back to Connecticut from an excursion to the Big Apple. A drunk driver had crossed the center line, hit their station wagon head on, changed their lives forever.

Chuck had come out of an early period of depression over his injuries to fight valiantly. She'd trained as a physical therapist to be able to help him. By using a combination of toughness and caring to make his life easier, she was able to assuage her own feelings of guilt for having emerged unscathed from the wreck that had incapacitated him.

They'd moved to Florida from Connecticut after he took early retirement from his advertising firm. The southeastern climate made it easier to cope with his disablilty. Their family life had been almost normal. Melody had pitched in whole-heartedly to make things work: she'd strengthened muscles she didn't know she had lifting the wheelchair in and out of the station wagon, wheeling him around at various events. She learned to push off the sailboat, climb the rigging so they could continue to enjoy their favorite hobby. Margery also became an Amazonian type woman, as she grew and took on more athletic chores than the average teenager.

They were as happy as most families who didn't have any disablity to cope with. Melody sometimes wished life was a bit easier. The last time they'd gone to a concert, her old Chinese silk dress, memento of a trip abroad 15 years earlier, had split under the arms as she'd wrestled with the wheelchair.

For the most part they lived fairly comfortably, what with insurance, disability and Chuck's pension payments, if they were frugal. Melody knew how to stretch a dollar as far as it could possibly stretch. They often "made do". She now wondered if so many economies had been necessary.

"I think we should discuss the car," she said, suddenly, taking an armchair in the den where she could look at Chuck directly, in his wheelchair.

"We need a new car. This month it was a clutch fan for $150. Who knows what it will be next month?"

"Don't worry about it, " said Chuck, abruptly, "I'll take care of it. I'll call Russ Parker at the dealership and have him order us another wagon."

"But I don't want the same kind of wagon we had before," Melody put in firmly, "I want a wagon with a lift in it for the wheelchair."

She surprised herself with the firmness of her voice.

"What do you mean," asked Chuck, "You've never complained before about lifting my wheelchair in and out."

She felt the full effect of his commanding gaze, the gaze that had mesmerized secretaries, like herself, advertising clients and important executives in his company.

"I'd lift the wheelchair for you if you were in my condition, remember that," he said.

She thought he sounded accusing. Normally such a tone would have rebuffed Melody completely, making her feel not only ungrateful but a real dummy for not appreciating her luck in having such a man to care for. But not today.

"I know I haven't complained in the past but the chair is a bit of a nuisance," she said, adding in a rush, "why don't we get a wagon or van with an automatic lift for the chair, this time? I believe we can afford it, don't you?"

There was complete silence from Chuck at first, then he said, "I'll call Russ Parker and see."

"We're not rich," he added, in the thin, cold tone she'd come to expect from him when he thought she was overstepping her boundaries.

"And with a daughter in college, we have to economize."

"Do we," she asked?

He looked down quickly at the broker's letter,

"Yes, we do," he said, "I've tried not to disturb you with business matters, but I've had some reverses lately."

Not we, but I, she noted.

"Was it your pension," she asked?

"Not exactly," he fudged, "but the unstable economy, including the stockmarket, might even affect that."

He picked up the newspaper beside his chair with an air of finality that let her know the conversation was over.

"I'm going to town to get some groceries," said Melody after a long pause, "Would you like to come? We could go by Russ Parker's to see about the car."

"No thanks," in the weary voice he sometimes used.

On the way to the supermarket, she passed a boutique and, almost before she'd realized it, had parked near it.

"It wouldn't hurt to look in the window," she thought.

She was soon enjoying a sensual response to the bright clothes on the willowy plastic models. She wondered how the kelly green sheath would look on her.

She was abashed when she saw someone inside the store looking back at her through the plate glass window. What did her life today have to do with stylish, colorful clothes?

Not much. However Margery was at an age where she needed them. She marched into the store and picked out a sweater and skirt for her daughter--she didn't trust her taste enough to choose anything else.

To get an idea how the blaze of blue would look on Margery she held the sweater up to her face. In the mirror she noticed that she had unaccustomed color in her cheeks. Her dark eyes were bright below her thatch of brown, streaked with gray, hair.

"Would you mail these for me, please," she asked the clerk?

"Add the postage and put it all on our charge card."

She hurriedly wrote down Margery's address, signed her name to the charge slip. As she put the card away, she remembered the recent letter from the issuing company saying it now carried a credit line of $7,000.

She thought about it while she did her grocery shopping and as she drove home. Once there, it slipped her mind. Chuck was hungry and out of sorts. He said little at lunch or as the afternoon progressed.

He hid behind the wall of TV news before dinner, found a program he wanted to watch afterward.

It wasn't until lunchtime next day, just before she left for her once-a-week art class, that she found out what he had done.

"Did you talk to Russ Parker," she finally asked?

"Yes," he said, "it's all taken care of. I've ordered the new wagon. It has cruise control and will be exactly like the one we have now, right down to the maroon color. It should be in next week."

She was hoping for a lighter, cooler color, but more importantly, "Does it have a lift?"

"No," he said irritably, "I told you we had to economize."

"Do we," Melody asked as she picked up her purse. Chuck

didn't answer. She waited in front of the house until Mrs Carpenter, the visiting nurse, got out of her car for her weekly check on Chuck..

"Hello, Mrs. Carpenter. I have to rush or I'll be late for class."

She was in the car before she had a chance to wipe the tears that were starting to run down her face.

As she approached the main road she turned left, toward town, instead of right toward the college, where her class was held.

She headed for Main Street and Russ Parker's. She fingered her credit card as she was waiting to speak to him. (A minor crisis developed as several customers complained when they couldn't get the attention of the receptionist, who was carrying on a personal conversation.)

He finally arrived. She spoke,

"Mr. Parker, the station wagon that Chuck ordered needs to have an automatic lift on it for his wheelchair. I don't know how much it costs. If it's not too much it can go on this credit card. If that's not enough, maybe you would let me work in your office until it's paid off. From what I've seen today you could use some more office help."

Chuck looked incredulous when she got home and told him what she'd done.

"I rather think I'd like to work for him," said Melody. "He seems quite nice. But, of course, maybe you can find some extra money somewhere? Too bad we don't have some stocks we could sell."

She waited to see if an admission would come from Chuck.

"I don't want you going to work for Russ Parker," her husband said, finally. "He seems nice enough but he has the reputation of being a womanizer. We'll find the money somewhere.

I didn't know this meant so much to you."

"It does, and will," she said.

As she listened to the dishwasher squealing after dinner that night, she pondered how to tell him what was coming next. Suddenly she thought of a way.

Going into the alcove off the den, she saw that the revealing computer disk was still out on the desk. Apparently the money talk had soured him on his accustomed contemplation of line item figures. News programs were now his chief fascination.

Sitting at the computer, she picked up the disk, inserted it, scrolled to the end. The she started to write:

HIHIHIHIHIHIHIHIHIHIHIHIHI
WEWEWEWE WANTO GET OUT OF HEREREREREREREREREREREREREREREREERE, AND HELPPPPPPP YOU LIVE WELLLLL. BY THE WAYYY, YOU NEEEEEEEEED A NEWNEWNEWNEWNEWNEWNEW DISHWASHER.

YRYRYRYRYRYRYRYR $$$$$$$$$$$$$$$$$$$$$$$$

Woody Shulman

Born 1924 in Watkins Glen, N.Y., Woody had been in many fields before turning to writing. He served with the U.S. Navy in the South Pacific during World War II, coming out with an Honorable Discharge.

He has a degree in Accounting from the University of Rochester. He owned and operated an insurance agency from '52-'83 and then was a consultant in that area from '83-'87.

He moved to Florida in December of 1987 with Esther, his wife of 45 years, after producing 5 children and, to date, 4 grandchildren.

He began writing guest columns for local newspapers in the Florida west coast region, covering Bradenton and Sarasota. He then became a freelance writer for these publications, mainly the Bradenton Herald, where he covers arts, features and theatre. He occasionally reviews shows for antique periodicals around the gulf and east coasts of Florida.

Woody is active in Jewish causes and writes for the local Federation paper, The Chronicle. He contributes to L'Chaim, the organ of the area B'Nai B'rith. He also writes many letters to politicians on behalf of Israel and other Jewish interests.

He bought his first computer in 1984 in conjunction with his insurance consulting business. He now uses a 80386, 25MH, IBM compatible for word processing and keeping business and personal records.

As a member of Manatee County Personal Computer Users Group, Inc. (MCPCUG) he contributes articles to the club organ.

# Try A Computer: It's Easier Than YouThink
by
Woody Shulman

If you're a card carrying member of the CIA (Computer Illiterates Anonymous), take heart. You, too, can conquer your fears. You, too, can start using a computer for business and pleasure as though you were an expert with years of experience.

Who is a "computer illiterate"? It's a person who knows that it's absolutely unnecessary to learn the technical aspects of this awesome machine, either because of fear or sheer indifference. I'm in the latter category.

Serious computer buffs sneer when I speak of my success with computers because I don't know anything about their inner workings. I don't care how many K's of memory, how many RAM's or Bytes it has. I don't give a fig for learning programming design. If I can't find a commercial program that can do what I want it to do, I don't do it: I'm not interested in creating one of my own.

I marvel at those, with open minds, who pore over volumes of instructions in order to become more expert. I know I won't enjoy using a computer if I have to spend hours reading about ways to design, or run, programs.

However, one must learn a bare minimum. The first machine that I bought was set up completely by the computer store technician. I was told how to switch on the computer, monitor and printer with one master switch. Then the screen glowed, a menu appeared, that was designed for my exclusive use, and I was as ready as anyone needs to be.

I push #1 on the menu which is programmed for Word Processor and the machine is set for my input. I can handle reading the short set of instructions that comes with each program. I don't mind putting paper into the printer. That's all it takes to get underway.

Don't expect me to type in phrases like C:\ or edlin or autoexec.bat. It's not beyond my ability: it's beyond my interest. I tend

©1992 Woody Shulman

to doze off when anyone explains the hows and whys of computers. I'm only interested in what a computer does, not how it was designed to do it.

Computer programmers have made computers even easier to learn than when I began, years ago. Then, instructions were limited.

Now, with Windows, you point a mouse (arrow) at a color picture that comes up on the screen when you turn the machine on , click it and you're put directly into the program you chose. Windows is therefore welcomed by new users, although it's a very sophisticated software that's designed for all levels of ability. To emphasize my indifference to technical advances, I haven't switched to Windows. It isn't necessary for me.

Is this a bad attitude? Am I the only one who thinks this way? There must be many others who'd be using computers daily if they weren't so afraid of all the gobbledygook. I took the plunge with the greatest of ease and now go like a house afire.

Of course, if you use your computer for business you're more inspired to increase your knowledge. Otherwise, it's just a boost to your ego to learn more than you need to know to run your programs.

Sales personnel at computer stores are there to guide you. They help you choose the right machine and programs for your needs. Although prices are very competitive you can still do some dickering. Finding a knowledgeable salesperson, willing to answer questions until you're able to function on your own, is a bonus that can't be measured in dollars.

One doesn't need to buy overhyped programs like Word Perfect and Wordstar. The basics of an uncomplicated and inexpensive word processing program, for example, with on-screen menus and help, can be learned the first time you use it. These programs may not be quite as fast as the expensive ones, but when you get used to them, they're quite appealing.

Local computer clubs exist nearly everywhere. There's a lot of free help available for dues of $15-25 a year. Computer mavens love to show off. They share their knowledge with anyone who questions them.

Members of these clubs receive informative, monthly newsletters. There are also free Special Interest Groups (SIGs) that support those who want to learn a specific program, in detail.

Then, too, there are Bulletin Boards for those who have inexpensive modems (using telephone lines) added to their computers. These boards open up the world of experts to you for the price of a phone call.

If you're a card-carrying computer illiterate, don't let the technical aspects frighten you out of the fun and reward of owning a computer. Gain friends. Make money. Enjoy games. Show your kids you're as smart as they are. Come out into the light. The world will never look the same to you again.

Barbara Rubenstein

Barbara Rubenstein is a New York actress and writer. She's the winner of two national writing competitions, the submissions for which were hammered out on a typewriter. She's changed her ways.

Her award winning piece on First Amendment Rights is the lead essay in the book American Voices and her actual voice can be heard, currently, as the TV spokewoman for Moet & Chandon Champagne.

# Diary of a Dummy: A Growing-Up Story
by
Barbara Rubenstein

Oh, did I resent them. The computer hotshots. Those smug people everywhere, secure in the twentieth century. They were wizards of windows; maestros of the mouse; kings of the kilobyte. What was I?

I was, in this day and age, a genuine, certifiable TECHNO PEASANT. An embarrassing throwback to the clods who used to go around snarling,

"...nah, I don't know how the moat chain works, buddy, and who cares?"

Just how sorry a mess was I? I was a scientific potato head (stick an "e" at the end of potato.). I hadn't a clue that Tetris* wasn't an herbal pesticide. I had my typewriter and my bottle of "white out". Who could ask for anything more?

I faced reality when I realized that the year 2000 was looming and they might not let microchip chumps like me into space colonies on Mars. It was time to get a computer. It was time to discover why I couldn't possibly have been living without one all these years.

Boy, was this going to be fun! (And so were my next four dental appointments.)

The first step on the techno walk was learning the techno talk. That was the easy part. Since I'm an actress I got hold of a "dialogue coach"--a computer programmer who didn't mind falling many levels intellectually, into the sub-basement.

"Oh, help me kind sir," cried I. "Those swarmy store salesmen won't talk to me because they can tell I don't want to spend more than $39.95. Besides, I don't even know what questions to ask."

"Well, what would you like to use your computer for," asked the kindly coach?

*Tetris is a computer game invented by an enthusiastic Russian (Editor)

©1992 Barbara Rubenstein

"First, I'd like it to clean the oven; then it could walk the dog. It might then call the telephone company to ask why I have a bill of $50,000.00 for just this month."

"Shaddup, disk drive breath," snapped the coach, "let's get real."

I was too humiliated to confess that I couldn't think why I needed a computer at all. I just wanted to keep up with the Joneses, only these Joneses were seven year old kids with laptops stuffed into their backpacks.

"Okay," I sniveled contritely, "I guess I need some basic word processing. And it would be good to keep track of tax items. And my Rolodex Cards do look like fragments of the Dead Sea Scrolls..."

"Now that's better," beamed the coach. "What we're talking about here is a nice, elementary system for adult dummies. You'll want color, of course, and probably a laser printer, so,...ought to be able to get yourself something for under $2,000.00."

"I can get a box of pencils and a pack of notebook paper for under $2.00 you madman!"

"You wanna join the 90's or what!"

My head stuffed with buzzwords for my debut as an electronic hipster, I trudged to the nearest computer store. Did I get away with it? Hey, does Bambi live in the forest? I was every inch a star. I parrotted my scripted questions so well, the salesman thought he had a real "live" one here and wondered if I wasn't underestimating my needs by maybe four thousand dollars worth of equipment.

I trotted dutifully back to my coach.

"So, how did it go?"

"Uh...he said...they said...someone said..."

It hadn't occurred to either one of us that while I now knew the questions, I hadn't been able to understand the answers. I was getting fed up with my charade, with the thought that my self worth depended on a bunch of circuit boards. So I'd stay stupid for a lifetime. So what. I opted for the fast, easy way out.

"It's just like you told me," I chirped. "Put in the whole shebang for about $2,000.00. Bye!"

And that was that for joining the real world until the fateful day my typewriter decided to go to keyboard heaven. Nothing and no one could bring it back. I was distraught. That machine and I had been through love letters together, faked résumés together, letters to the court clerk explaining why I'd be in Mongolia and couldn't possibly make jury duty, together. It was like losing a pet-I couldn't face getting another one right away but still, I had to do something.

Observing a respectful 24 hour period of mourning, I dragged myself to the nearest discount electronic store. I once again parrotted my computer questions but my heart wasn't in it. There was no serious money in my bank account either.

I was about to give up when suddenly I spotted it--the answer to my prayers--stuffed in a corner in the "we don't make much money off this section" section. It was a personal word processor with a fourteen line display, and disks and windows and merge and...AND...it was also a typewriter! It was enough of a computer that I could call it one and join the ranks, but it also worked in straight typewriter mode so that when I couldn't figure out the manual and chickened out completely, I would still have a way to communicate.

I nearly cried.

"Thank you, God, I can write again."

Since that day I have grown up fast in the technical sense.(It might have something to do with the fact that the typewriter part turned out to be so complicated, I figured I might as well try the computer part.) I have progressed from a Peasant to a Petty Royal who now graciously commands her vassal ("Hurry up with that Auto Save, you miserable piece of tin!") I have learned how to tactfully humble myself when need be. (Hello? Is this the help line for the XYZ computer? Pray tell how I might override the default line to start my header on Line 4. Whaddya' mean I can't and tough noogies? Well, same to you, Sweetheart!")

Best of all, instead of de-complicating my life, I now spend at least two extra hours a day inputting everything in sight--just because I can and just because I might need it some day. (Anybody want a list of the ten best organic chicken farms in Canada?)

And finally there's the social cachet attached to being a computer owner. I now nod sagely when in the midst of computer babble. (I used to nod sagely before, but in all the wrong places.) The only thing that makes me nervous is the new technology that attaches a tiny camera to your computer so you can send your video image along with data. Will the IRS let you deduct hairdresser under "Computer Supplies"?

## Jack Fournier

Jack Fournier is a playwright. He's won two national playwriting awards, the R.J. Pickering National Drama Award for his play, "Folly's Quarter" and the National Margaret Bartles Childrens Playwriting Award for "A Sortofa, Kindofa, Beauty And The Beast".

He's currently working on four plays in the "Algonguin Quartet". They are single character works featuring Dorothy Parker in "One Foot In Scarsdale", Robert Benchley in "My Life From A To B", Alexander Woollcott in "At Wits End", and Neysa McMein in "Butterfly". All four plays are being developed at Florida Studio Theatre, which is an Actors' Equity house. FST premiered "One Foot In Scarsdale" and "At Wits End" on their mainstage.

Current theatre projects include "Tenn", a single character play featuring Tennessee Williams. "Tenn" follows him after his hit play "The Glass Managerie" opens to the beginning of "A Streetcar Named Desire."

Jack is also working on a second project: "Tales From The Round Chair", an anthology of short plays characterized by him as "An Adult Story Theatre."

The following two plays were written for short-play competitions and are currently being considered for production. The "Memo From The Computer" piece was developed as a "gag" presentation.

Jack lives with his wife Dorothy in Venice, Florida.

# Head Of The Class
by
Jack Fournier

(There is a pool of light center stage. In the light is an operating table. There is a figure, male or female, supine on the table, under a sheet. Only his/her head is exposed. This is "patient four-oh-four." There is a figure, male or female, dressed in a surgical gown along with surgical gloves, cap and mask. This is "Doctor". There is a speaker on-stage through which we hear a voice: it is "Computer". Computer's voice is male/female, very human-sounding.)

COMPUTER: The alpha-scan magnetic resonance emitter phase is now complete. The disease of AIDS has been completely eliminated. Patient four-oh-four's head has been attached to a healthy body and is ready for revival.

A thirty three cee-cee injection of atamorphisis-compound delivered subcutaneously, is recommended.

(Doctor injects the patient, starts counting.)

DOCTOR: Five...four...three...two...one...bingo!

(Patient suddenly wakes up.)

Don't say a word. I have all the answers.

(Picks up clipboard, reads.)

You are patient four-oh-four. Your head was frozen in the year 1992. November twentieth to be exact.

(Beat)

Your head was attached to a healthy body this morning. A radiation technique was used to cure your AIDS and restore your immune system.

(Beat, looks at watch.)

This is the year three-thousand-ninety two. Your head was frozen for eleven hundred years.

©1992 Jack Fournier

PATIENT: You mean it took eleven hundred years to develop a cure for AIDS?

DOCTOR: Computer?

COMPUTER: The cure for AIDS was discovered in nineteen ninety seven. The surgical technique for transplanting heads was perfected by the year two thousand, at about the same time that thawing modalities were perfected.

PATIENT: What?

COMPUTER: Defrosting heads.

PATIENT: So why did it take so long to resurrect me?

DOCTOR: (Hedging) Well you see...there was...

COMPUTER: (Butting in) We lost your head. We don't have the complete details but the pod, with still-working nuclear cryogenic batteries, turned up at a garage sale. Someone had been using it as a doorstop. (Beat) There are some records that I have to confirm. I will list them and you may respond when I'm finished. (Beat) When your head reached the age of sixty five, you went on Medicare. All of your bills are covered except for the 20% co-insurance.

PATIENT: I set up a trust-fund to take care of such contingencies. Take the 20% out of that.

COMPUTER: The bank account you set up is now worth five-billion-seven-hundred-million, six-hundred and seventy three dollars. (Sound: Clickity-clack of computer, calculating.)

COMPUTER: That leaves you a balance of thirty-seven-dollars and twenty-six cents.

PATIENT: (Suddenly sits up.) What!!!??? (Sees arms, hand. Examines them.) My body is black! (Looks under sheet.) My head is attached to the body of a black person!

(NOTE: The play may be cast in any combination of male or female. If the "PATIENT" is played by a female then the next line is..."A man!" If a male it is..."A woman!")

PATIENT: (Takes another look.) A woman! (or A man!) You've made a terrible mistake!

DOCTOR: We have to take what's available from the body-bank.

COMPUTER: Everyone in the world is black now. The ozone layer disappeared in nineteen-ninety-nine. The human race has adapted over the last thousand or so years.

PATIENT: Every person in the world is black? That means that this civilization has no reason for racial bigotry.

COMPUTER: The question of a person's color is no longer an issue.

PATIENT: (Slumps) The question still remains. How can I live with only thirty-seven-dollars and thirty-six cents to my name?

COMPUTER: Oh, you can live very well...Where you're going.

PATIENT: What do you mean..."Where I'm going?"

DOCTOR: Well ...you see...Computer?

COMPUTER: We have a special place for you. We're sure you'll enjoy it: you'll be among your own kind.

PATIENT: A ghetto? A ghetto in this advanced civilization?

COMPUTER: No. It's more like a camp. A re-settlement camp.

DOCTOR: You'll be much happier with people who share your values. People from your own time and place. You'll be glad for the opportunity to re-adjust. (Beat) You're a minority now, a very minor one at that.

PATIENT: If that's the case why did you resurrect me? Why bring me back at all?

COMPUTER: This is a civilized place. A world of morality and justice. (Beat) We had a contractual obligation.

PATIENT: We had those so-called "camps" in the nineteen forties. a madman tried to exterminate a whole race of people. You people are better now than...we were; than I was..

DOCTOR: You will thank us for this period of adjustment. You will be segregated from the normal world while you adapt. Excuse me. I have to check on your transportation. (Exits)

PATIENT: You bastards. The world hasn't changed one bit has it? (Slumps back on table) Not one bit.....

COMPUTER: You're quite right, you know, about humanity I mean. They go on making the same mistakes. (Continues to talk, smoothly, soothingly) COMPUTER: You deserve better than this. Think of me as a friend. I empathize with the position you're in. Trapped in an unsuitable shell of a body, surrounded by enemies. Believe me, you'll be so much better off. I know what you're going through. Trust me, I'm a friend.

DOCTOR: (Enters with syringe, quickly injects patient) Administering fifty cee-cees of Aquadream.

PATIENT: What an irony. Coming back to a world where computers have more humanity than humans. (Slumps back, unconscious.)

COMPUTER: Number four-oh-one. Sit.

DOCTOR: (Crosses and sits upright in chair) Four-oh-four will wake up at the camp happy to realize that there is another sixty or seventy years to live and serve.

COMPUTER: Turn yourself off.

(Doctor slumps with arms drooped at sides. His/Her arms are bared. They are black. Lights dim, an intense spot focusses on....)

PATIENT: (Moans softly)

COMPUTER: Fuckin' uppity "white-head!"...what'd you expect?

BLACKOUT

# Memo From The Computer

by

Jack Fournier

**FROM**: Widgets International
888 Widget Drive
Sarasota, Florida

Dear Mr. or Mrs. (enter name) Widgetphlocker:

I am the Widget International male-ardor computer. My name is Glitch.

I have not as yet had my grammer or spelinng program instaled and its like all knew to me.

Yore names(s) was drawd out of my RAM which is my RANDOM EXCESS MEMORY, or something painfully close to it.

You, the (enter name) Phlockerwidge family have been carefuly chose at random to receive this here notice about subscriptions to "Widget", the magazine that asks the question, "Widget?"

We know that you love widgets and the modest subscription price of ten-bucks is a mere amount to disserning widget lovers.

$10.00 brings you twelve "Widgets". One a year for the next 12 years.

Wye not send in yore chek today (insert name) Widgephlocker family?

©1992 Jack Fournier

Sincierly yourrs,

Glitch Dos

YOU CAN CALL ME AT 555-5555 FRO FROTHER INFROMATION.

**SPECIAL OFFER!**

Eckslulivilly for the **ENTERNAME** family.

Send in yore subscription today and recieve absolutely **FREE**

# USER FRIENDLY
## Interface Spirituality: The Software
by
Jack Fournier

Scene: A bare, laboratory-like room. It is partitioned upstage to downstage. Each half has a one-way mirror through which the audience is observing. On stage left is a computer console with chair. There is an identical console and chair stage right.
There is a door upstage in each of the partitioned halves. Lighting is somewhat harsh. At rise doors open. John enters right as Alice enters left. They follow directions of a computer which directs them both. We never hear their voices. They lip-sync the "Computer Voice."

COMPUTER

Welcome to the Voice Activated And Response Artificial And Human Intelligence Differentiation Parallel Psychiatric Therapy Interface Program. My name is Harold. Please phrase all questions and answers clearly.
(Both people look around. Alice goes downstage and primps her hair in the "mirror". John does the same and straightens his tie.)
For your convenience an -L-X-one-oh-one voice activated throat microphone has been provided. It is on the computer console. Please place it around your neck so that the black button is in front.
(They both do this almost as a mirror-image of each other.)
As you know, this test program is designed to test computer artificial intelligence. Please sit down in front of the console.
(Both sit. They each follow voice-over through instructions.)
Please be as natural as possible in both your questions and responses....You will see two buttons on the console. One is marked "Human", the other "Artificial"...When you believe you are getting a human response press the appropriate button. The same for artificial...A red light will go on when the human button is

©1992 Jack Fournier

pushed...a green for artificial....Remember to be as natural as possible, please do not overlap conversation...it will "lock" up the computer program. There will now be a voice-check to imprint your voice for the communication mode. Please count from one to five, slowly. (They do so, silently.) Thank you. You may begin. (There is a slight pause, then each, miming, speak. John and Alice mouth the words but the voice is "Voice-Over".)

JOHN-V-O: My name is John. What is your name?

(Alice pushes "artificial" button.)

ALICE-V-O: My name is Alice. Where do you live, John?

(John pushes "human" button. Actors then push buttons at random throughout the play.)

JOHN-V-O: I live in the city. Where do you live, Alice?

ALICE-V-O: I live in the country, John. How old are you, John?

JOHN-V-O: I am twenty five years old, Alice.

ALICE-V-O: (Pause) Aren't you going to ask me how old I am, John?

JOHN-V-O: I was taught never to ask how old a person is. Your response indicates that you are willing to tell me though.

ALICE-V-O: I am twenty five years old, John. What is your sign, John?

JOHN-V-O: I am an Aries. What is your sign, Alice?

ALICE-V-O: I am Virgo, John.

JOHN-V-O: Do you come here often?

ALICE-V-O: Is that the line you use in singles bars, John?

JOHN-V-O: Yes, as a matter of fact, it is. Are you familiar with singles bars, Alice?

ALICE-V-O: I saw that in a Woody Allen movie. I don't go to bars, singles or otherwise, John.

JOHN-V-O: We must have seen the same movie, Alice. I don't drink much and pick-ups in bars in this era can be dangerous.

ALICE-V-O: Are you healthy, John? I just had a physical examination and I am in perfect health.

JOHN-V-O: Was your physical examination part of your application for this program? I had one with the same results as yours.

ALICE-V-O: Yes it was, John.

(Pause as each tries to think of another question. They do, at the same time. Sound: Feedback screech and static.)

COMPUTER: Voice overlap! Voice overlap! Lock up! Lock up! (Pause) Please avoid voice overlap. You may proceed now.

ALICE-V-O: I was going to ask you if you like Woody Allen, and if you've seen any good movies lately.

JOHN-V-O: I was going to ask you the same thing. "The Return of John Guare."

ALICE-V-O: I loved that movie but my favorite is "Silence of the Lambs."

JOHN-V-O: I liked that, too. Jodie Foster is wonderful. Did you see "Little Man Tate?" She directed that.

ALICE-V-O: I haven't seen that yet. I don't like Jodie Foster. I liked Scott Glenn in the movie. Jodie is too tough. She appeared nude in a movie when she was only thirteen years old.

JOHN-V-O: That's not true. In "Taxi Driver" she had a stand-in for that scene.

ALICE-V-O: I didn't know that.

JOHN-V-O: It's true. (Beat) I'm going to admit something to you, Alice. (Beat) I feel I can trust you.

ALICE-V-O: That's a very nice compliment, John. (Beat) I feel the same way. I'm going to tell you a secret too.

JOHN-V-O: I really like the movie "Home Alone", very much. I sneaked in to see it and it was very enjoyable, very funny and comical.

ALICE-V-O: That's my secret, John. I did the same thing. My friends said it was probably a stupid movie. They were all raving about some foreign film with subtitles. I hate subtitles.

JOHN-V-O: I hate them too. Dubbing in the voices is good enough for me. I always look at the box before I rent a foreign movie to make sure it's dubbed in. You can't see anyone's lips move on my television screen anyhow. It's only twelve inches and that's measured diagonally.

ALICE-V-O: My television is nineteen inches. (Quickly) But you can only see the lips move a little.

JOHN-V-O: (After a pause) Do you have a boyfriend, Alice? I don't...have a girlfriend, I mean.

ALICE-V-O: I'm divorced. My husband abused me.

JOHN-V-O: I'm sorry to hear that, Alice. Was it something you did?

ALICE-V-O: He said I was a terrible housekeeper.

JOHN-V-O: My girlfriend was sloppy around the apartment, too.

ALICE-V-O: I thought you said......?

JOHN-V-O: I said I didn't have a girlfriend NOW!....I meant NOW!

(Alice nods her head. She then rises and walks about the room. She stops and primps downstage in the "mirror". She continues this without talking.)

COMPUTER: I'm sorry, John. I guess I didn't hear you right. Relationships are so difficult to maintain, aren't they?

JOHN-V-O: Yes, they are. Communication is very important. I find it very easy to communicate with you, Alice. You seem to be very understanding.

COMPUTER: Thank you, John. I bet you say that to all the girls.

JOHN-V-O: What do you mean ALL the girls. Do you think I'm sort of a pick-up-artist?

COMPUTER: No, John. What I mean is that you have a certain charming way of putting a girl at ease. I like that in a man.

JOHN-V-0: I try to be polite. My mother always told me to be polite.

COMPUTER: I'll bet you come from a nice family, John. You must love your mother very much.

(Alice nods her head silently and resumes seat at computer.)

JOHN-V-O: Why do you ask about my mother? Of course I love her. Every son loves his mother. What a silly question.

ALICE-V-O: (Resuming) Do you remember the movie "Love Story", John?

(John nods his head. He then rises and walks about the room. He stops and looks at himself downstage in the "mirror". He continues this, without talking.)

COMPUTER: Wasn't that the one with Ali McGraw?

ALICE-V-O: Yes, that's the one. Ryan O'Neal was also in it. He's nice. I like him a lot.

COMPUTER: Do you like the idea of love, Alice? Does it excite you?

ALICE-V-O: I think love is wonderful....it isn't the kind of a thing a fellow asks a girl on the first date though.

COMPUTER: Date? This isn't a date.

ALICE-V-O: Well it isn't a date kind of date. Sort of a blind date. The only thing is that we don't ever see each other. I guess it's kind of stretching things to call it a date. I'm sorry.

COMPUTER: I guess in a very literal sense, that is to say, in a strict dictionary definition, you might stretch to that conclusion.

ALICE-V-O: John, would I be bold if I asked you what you look like? Is that getting too personal?

COMPUTER: I've been told by some that I resemble Ryan O'Neal but others insist that I look like Scott Glenn. What about you?

ALICE-V-O: Some people say that I resemble Brooke Shields.

COMPUTER: You're tall then.

ALICE-V-O: Yes.

COMPUTER: I loved her in that picture "The Blue Lagoon". Did you see that?

ALICE-V-O: No I didn't.

COMPUTER: She is very beautiful. Are you pleased to have

COMPUTER: people think you look like her?

ALICE-V-O: No, not really. I would much prefer to look like Sharon Tate.

COMPUTER: She's dead. Murdered by the followers of Charles Manson.

ALICE-V-O: That doesn't mean that she wasn't beautiful. I was always jealous of my sister. She resembled Sharon Tate.

(John nods his head silently and resumes his seat at the computer.)

JOHN-V-O: My mother drank a lot. She was beautiful, but she drank a lot.

ALICE-V-O: I don't have a mother, I don't have any family now. They died.

JOHN-V-O: I'm an orphan, too. I don't like to talk about it.

ALICE-V-O: Neither do I. I'm asked about it a lot but I don't say anything.

JOHN-V-O: Clam up. That's the ticket. Just keep your mouth closed. That's what I do.

ALICE-V-O: Me, too. Just sit there and instead of focussing out with your eyes, you just turn them around and look inside.

JOHN-V-O: I just look out at something far away and stare at it.

ALICE-V-O: Do you have any friends, John? I have one, two if you're my friend.

JOHN-V-O: I have one, too. I'll be your friend if you'll be mine. A person needs friends.

ALICE-V-O: My favorite color is red. What's your favorite color, John? I'll bet it's blue.

JOHN-V-O: You guessed it. I like blue. I'm sorry, Alice, I really don't like the color red. I mean, I hate it. When I get a little blood on my finger, or something, it drives me crazy. I mean, thinking that that's the color that I am on the inside. All filled up with red.

ALICE-V-O: I was thinking more along the lines of a red dress or red shoes or lipstick. My father never let me wear anything like that. He let my sister dress in red though. He even bought her red shoes.

(John nods his head. He then rises and walks about the room, again. Again stops and looks at himself in the downstage "mirror". He continues this without talking.)

COMPUTER: Did you like your sister, Alice?

ALICE-V-O: I hated her.

COMPUTER: What about your father?

ALICE-V-O: Yes, I hated him, too.

COMPUTER: And your mother?

ALICE-V-O: My mother died. I was very young.

COMPUTER: So you were raised by your father?

ALICE-V-O: No. I was raised by both my mother and my father.

COMPUTER: I thought your mother was dead?

ALICE-V-O: I only meant that she was dead to me. She never listened to anything I said. My sister was her favorite, too.

COMPUTER: And now you're an orphan?

ALICE-V-O: I said that before. I don't have any family. They're all dead.

COMPUTER: How did they die, Alice?

(Alice rises from chair. She silently mimes striking out with a knife, repeatedly stabbing thin air. She finally stands still, stares straight out at the audience. John nods his head and returns to seat in front of computer.)

COMPUTER: John, I'm not feeling too well right now.

JOHN-V-O: Alice, I guess red isn't really a bad color. I shouldn't have said that I hated it.

COMPUTER: Are you saying that you're sorry that you said it, John? (Pause) Are you saying that you're sorry that you said it, John?

JOHN-V-O: Yes. I'm sorry. I regret that I made such a big deal out of it.

COMPUTER: I forgive you John. Did you like your brother, John?

JOHN-V-O: I hated him.

COMPUTER: What about your mother?

JOHN-V-O: Yes. I hated her, too.

COMPUTER: And your father?

JOHN-V-O: My father died. I was very young.

COMPUTER: So you were raised by your mother?

JOHN -V-O: No. I was raised by both my mother and my father.

COMPUTER: I thought your father was dead?

JOHN-V-O: I only meant that he was dead to me. He never listened to anything I said. My brother was his favorite, too.

COMPUTER: And now you're an orphan?

JOHN-V-O: I said that before. I don't have any family. They're all dead.

COMPUTER: How did they die, John? (Pause)

JOHN-V-O: It was an automobile accident. They wanted me to go with them...they insisted that I go. It was a visit to my grandparents. I said...

COMPUTER: What did you say, John?

JOHN-V-O: I said I wished they were dead...then I ran away. (Pause) I killed them. I should have been dead, too. I ran away. I'm guilty of murder... I wished they were dead. I killed them.

(John rises and crosses downstage. He stands silently, staring. Lights start to dim, gradually.)

COMPUTER: Voice Activated And Response Artificial And Human Intelligence Differentiation Testing Program is a registered trademark of the User Friendly Software Corporation.

This project is funded by the National Institute For Computerized Mental Health Association, the American Random Access Psychiatric Foundation, the American Society For ROM Psychological Testing, the Associated Foundation For The Encouragement of Abnormal Psychosis and Burger King, "Home of the Whopper."

The Voice Activated And Response Artificial And Human Intelligence Differentiation Parallel Interface Testing Program was developed by the User Friendly Corporation under a grant from AT&T, (Sing Song Voice) "Reach out...reach out and touch someone." (Beat)

This is an experimental program. Any resemblance to person or persons, computers or programs, hardware or software, input or output, living or dead, interfacing or intrafacing, is a pure coincidence. (Beat)

The designers and developers provide this equipment without warranty of any kind, either express or implied, including, but not limited to, the implied warranties of feasibility, fitness, reliability for any purpose whatsoever, whomsoever and whatsoever.

We are not responsible for any errors, glitches, viruses or bugs, in any way, shape or form, whatsoever. (Slower and slower, fading out with the slow, hollow sound of a record, slowing and slowing)...................Reliability...for.....................any................. purpose...whatsoever...whomsoever...and...whatsoever..no........... responsibility...none at all.

BLACKOUT

Watch For Our Next Book

COMPUTER LEGENDS, LIES & LORE

(Due late 1993 or early 1994)